A ROMANCE
IN THE FIELDS

A ROMANY
IN THE FIELDS

G. BRAMWELL EVENS
(THE ROMANY OF THE B.B.C.)

LARGE PRINT
Oxford

Copyright © G. Bramwell Evens, 1929

First published in Great Britain 1929
by
The Epworth Press

Published in Large Print 2006 by ISIS Publishing Ltd.,
7 Centremead, Osney Mead, Oxford OX2 0ES
by arrangement with
the Author's Estate

British Library Cataloguing in Publication Data
Evens, George Bramwell, 1884–1943
   A Romany in the fields. – Large print ed.
   (Isis reminiscence series)
   1. Natural history – Great Britain
   2. Country life – Great Britain
   3. Large type books
   I. Title
   508.4'1

ISBN 0–7531–9316–7 (hb)
ISBN 978–0–7531–9317–4 (pb)

Printed and bound in Great Britain by
T. J. International Ltd., Padstow, Cornwall

DEDICATED TO

MY WIFE

without whose inspiration this book would
not have been written.

"God's finger touched, but did not press,
In making England."

A ROMANY IN THE FIELDS

in which Raq and I introduce you to:

JOHN FELL	*Gamekeeper*
JERRY	*Poacher*
ALAN AND JOE	*Farmers*
NED	*Village Postman*
JOHN RUBB	*Angler*

———

The dialect is not that of any particular district, rather have I tried to catch something of the quaintness of country dialogue which will be understood in the North and in the South.

CONTENTS

AUTUMN

The Balance of Nature

I ought to say at once that I am a "tramp" by choice and not of necessity. Lingering in the city either to gaze at shop-windows, or to be regularly amused by some "show," is not my highest form of bliss.

I prefer to loiter in green meadows, to explore the fringes of quiet pools and the margins of laughing streams, to muse under shadowed hedges — in a word, to potter about where the wild birds sing or where the trout rises to the fly.

As a companion, I have my dog Raq. I take him, firstly, because a spaniel is the most lovable and sensible thing on four legs, and, secondly, because the alliance between my sight and his nose is a very strong one. What I miss in the bushes he points out. He stands like a statue before any discovery, his eyes questioning mine, and, according to the interest of his find, even so works his stubby tail. Should it be a hare lying snug in its "form," then his tail works fast and furious; if it be a mouse, then a few mild jerks is quite sufficient for the occasion.

It was with him that I found myself one morning walking along a path which leads through a wood. Like a well-trained dog, he trotted contentedly at my heels.

On all sides the quietness of those shadowed aisles was broken by the protests of those who resented our intrusion. A pair of jays were not only resentful, but positively abusive, and hurled at us every epithet in their bird vocabulary. I saw the flash of their saxe-blue markings as they dodged behind the hazel-bushes.

Farther on, the wood-pigeons, sometimes called "cushats" or "queece," launched themselves from the pines, and, in order to give warning of our approach, clapped their raised wings with resounding smacks.

Even the wren was annoyed by our progress, and creaked out her petulance as we penetrated deeper into her sanctuary.

Finally we reached our objective — a small hut in a clearing, and here we waited.

The dog lay down at my feet. How differently each of us got into touch with the world around us! I was limited to what I could see and touch. Even my hearing could not be compared with his.

I watched his moist muzzle. Now it twitched to the right, and he knew that a pheasant was moving in the distant undergrowth. Now it veered to the left, and told him of a rabbit that lay crouching in its "seat" under the blackberry-bush.

Then he raised his head, and his tail, working slowly at first, nearly wagged itself off as there came to my ears the steps of him whom I sought as he made his way to the hut.

I would like you to meet John Fell; that is, if you are on legitimate business, for he is the gamekeeper of the estate.

There are gamekeepers and gamekeepers. Some there are who only know their own particular line of business. They know how to rear a few pheasants, they can level a gun at what they call "vermin," and perchance can train a dog. But John knew the call of every bird, could interpret every track left in sand or mud, and was a sure hand at branding everything with feather or fur on it, as friend or foe. He had only two hobbies — his work and his Church.

"Anything fresh?" was his greeting to me.

This did not mean that he wished to hear an epitome of the morning's paper.

"Well," said I, "there's a heifer calf arrived this morning at Whiterigg; during the night a fox has killed two ducks and seven pullets of Jim Doyle's; and I saw them up at the Blue Farm starting to thatch."

He nodded appreciatively.

"Ye've an eye and an ear for the country," he said; and, seeing that he was in a good humour, I offered him my pouch. (This was good strategy on my part to get him to sit down and have a crack.) But he shook his head, and said, with a smile:

"I like a smoke," and forthwith he proceeded to cut, from a fearsome-looking slab, slices of black tobacco.

Whilst he was filling his pipe I was gazing at the side of the hut, against which were suspended a few carrion crows, magpies, sparrow-hawks, and an odd stoat or two.

"How is it," I asked, pointing to the ramshackle carcasses, "that you shoot so few of what keepers call 'vermin'? I have seen scores of stoats, weasels, kestrels, owls, and sparrow-hawks outside other keepers' huts; you have the poorest show of any I know."

"Well," said John, taking a deep pull at his pipe, "I believe in the balance o' Natur'."

I sat silent, as I knew he loved to open out a phrase,  and I also knew that if he were not in a talking mood nothing would induce him to open out.

"The balance o' Natur'," he continued, "is a pecoolier thing. Some as don't believe in it. I do."

He picked up a straight twig, laying it at right angles across his first finger, as though to illustrate his words.

"Ye see that bit o' wood?" he asked, looking at me from underneath shaggy brows. "It's lyin' straight now, 'cos both sides are equal. I shove this side a bit, ye see, and t'other 'un cocks up. I've made a mess o' the balance."

I nodded, knowing that he hated to have his moods fractured.

"So it is with Natur'," he said. "Everything alive, if we but knew it, balances one another. Rats'll eat partridges, and partridge chicks. But the weasels and stoats come along and kill the rats. Mice come along and do a deal o' damage to cornstacks, but the owls come out at the rising of the moon and pick up thousands of mice. The sparrerhawk snatches the small birds from the hedges, but we should be owerrun with 'em if they didn't. Shoot all the swallers to-morrer, and what'll ye do with the insects swarm next season? I'm speakin', o' course, in a general way."

6

For answer I took up a straight twig, and, as it lay on my finger, cocked up one side more than the other.

He smiled and added, "That's what 'ud happen on this estate if I shot every weasel or stoat that popped up in front of my gun. No doubt they take a few eggs, and perhaps a few chicks, but, if ye haven't too many about the place, they pay for their keep. Destroy the nateral enemies of the rats and mice if yer like — but ye have to pay the price o' their increase."

After I was sure that he had finished, I said:

"That reminds me of something you may have heard of. A few years ago the farmers in Scotland were alarmed at the appearance of a plague of voles. There were hundreds of thousands of them. All their crops suffered, and it seemed as though they would all be ruined.

"So threatening was the menace that the Government was appealed to, and they tried to discover some means of coping with the plague. But, before they were ready, Nature found her own remedy.

"Into the devastated districts there came swarms of the fiercest enemies of the voles. The owls came in their hundreds. The little red hunters, the weasels, ran amuck amongst them; kestrels poised in mid-air, made their relentless swoops. What the Government could not do, talon and beak, tooth and claw, did. And the result?"

Here I simply pressed down the cocked-up end of the twig and restored it to the level on my finger.

John smiled delightedly at the story and its confirmation of his own ideas.

"Ye talk about yer wireless," he said. "How did those owls and hawks know that there was abundance of food for 'em in Scotland? Who sent the S.O.S. to the weasels and the stoats?" He paused for a moment." "There's a text fer ye — 'Whithersoever the body is, thither will the eagles be gathered together'."

The keeper's pipe was out and his chat ended. "So long," he said, and, with firmly planted strides. went off to his duties.

"Cheerio," I replied. "See you again soon."

When I was alone I turned to the dog, and as I began to speak he sat up and looked at me with soulful eyes, whilst his noble head, with its long ears, reminded me of the pictures of Egyptian Rameses.

"Raq, my lad," said I, "you have just listened to a phrase which contains a good deal of wisdom, and I hope you took it all in."

The dog's tail began to wag furiously. He might not be able to understand what I was saying, but he liked its bantering, caressing tone.

"The Balance of Nature — that's the theme. It hints that the universe is run on a compensating system. If anything lacks something, then some other thing is added to keep the twig level. 'What you lose on the swings you make up on the roundabouts', as Aristotle or Harry Lauder says. If you have a wet summer you may still get good root crops, turnips and mangels; if dry, then a decent harvest of hay and corn."

"Also," I added as an afterthought, "if you are in a wide country circuit you have more travelling about than if you are in a town circuit, but in a town circuit you have to make more new sermons per quarter — there it is, the Balance of Nature, as plain as a pikestaff."

As I walked on I kept that phrase before me. A thrush poured out its heart from an elm and a kingfisher flashed, like an emerald, up stream. The former is not much to look at, but what a voice! The latter has no voice, only a grating "Zit, zit," but what robes! I applied the gamekeeper's idea, and found it illuminating.

A little later we sat down together to enjoy our lunch — it was Monday's fare — a few sandwiches made of cold meat. At home we should have turned up our noses at it or had a poor appetite.

But how different is its flavour when you eat it sprayed with the lark's music, seasoned with the curlew's plaintive pipe, and scented with the wild thyme which blows from the fells.

Then my eyes fell on a paragraph in the paper which had been a wrapper for my lunch. It stated that a big prize was being offered to any gardener who could produce a rose that was not only stately in poise, fine in texture, and royal in bloom, but possessed a fragrance. Evidently it was difficult to coax Nature to endow one rose with all the qualities of colour and scent. If it had magnificent petals, then it lacked the languid odour that the ragged white roses possess which grow in profusion over cottage doors. Here evidently the gamekeeper's idea was again being verified.

"Aye, Raq, my boy," said I, turning to my faithful companion, "that's a grand phrase — the Balance of Nature. It speaks to me of the stars in their courses, of wind and tide, of summer and winter, of garlands and wreaths, of the sorrow that comes at night and of the joy which breaks with the dawn, of life — of death."

I paused for a moment, and then quoted quietly to myself, "For God hath set the one over against the other."

Just so; the Balance of Nature is but another name for the equipoise of God.

The Interwoven Fabric

There is a brown tweed suit that hangs in my wardrobe that I love. It is nothing to look at. The coat is patched in various places, but they are honourable scars, and are souvenirs of stirring days. That one by the elbow speaks of a perilous climb on solitary Ailsa Craig, where the chant of the gannets nearly became a dirge. That darn on the left pocket reminds me that it is not the best of places in which to slip a young weasel. That dark stain — But I must not linger with such reminiscences or I shall never put it on.

How easily it slips on, and how glorious is its musty, peaty flavour! I feel wrapped in heather. Moreover, I contrast it with those other dark suits which I have left hanging in the wardrobe. They speak of meetings, official gatherings, conventional unnaturalness. When I don them I am supposed to be religiously attired; they tyrannize over me and forbid me to sit on anything less dignified than a chair, or lean against anything less sedate than a desk. But this

11

old brown tweed flecked with blue says to me, "The lanes are calling. Take me through hedges, wade with me through streams. Sit where you like, in grass or on stubble. I will fade you into the landscape so that the hawk shall not see you. I will mask you in the bracken so that the fox will pass you by." That old suit is the wedding garment to the feast of the wild.

There is one other, also, who loves it as I do. When I make my appearance in it, Raq, the spaniel, curls back his lips with delight, and so far forgets his training as to give a bark.

Then he watches me slip my binoculars on to my back, and waits for me to upset the whole household with, "Where's my waterproof bag?" "Where did I put my leggings?" "Where's the fly-cast I left in my hat?" And he invariably listens to the same reply, always given, too, with the same chilly sweetness, "They are where you left them, dear."

Strange, how I can find anything in a wood and nothing in a house. Probably it is because I do not look for them. At least, that is what I am told — every time.

Soon the city is left far behind, and we three — myself, my brown suit, and my dog — are strolling through an old-world village. The old clothes bring me close to every villager I meet. I think of those creased horrors that lie smugly at home. Were I wearing them, every labourer would pass me by on the other side of the street, and the children would sidle behind their cottage-doors, or stop their frolics until the shadow had passed.

But now it is "Good morning, Sam" — "Hullo, Mary" — there are no Mr. and Mrs. in the village. Every one knows each other intimately. Every genealogical tree is common property.

"Aye," they say, with a rising, lazy inflection of the voice, "I know Nancy Morton. She's Ben Tavistock's bairn. She has a brother livin' up at Kelvin and a sister wed to Ted Thorn, the veterinary. The brother's not up to much, I reckon, but Nancy makes a good wife — a good 'un."

And so, in this friendly, leisurely atmosphere, I pass through the High Street until at last in the distance I catch sight of a familiar figure. Raq, too, has got wind of him, and we hurry to overtake the postman on his daily round.

"Good morning, Ned," I call as I draw near.

"Marnin', sir," says he. That "sir" is merely a tribute to the coat and collar I have left at home. There is not a touch of servility in it.

Ned, I may say, is quite a character, and has a philosophy of life all his own. He has insight as well as sight, and nothing escapes his keen vision as he tramps from farm to farm.

After we have passed a few remarks concerning the crops and the price of cattle, I casually remark: "And what have you been thinking of lately?" This is quite a stock question of mine, for I know the old man is always working out some definite theme in his own mind.

"I have bin thinkin'," (here he stopped and took hold of my coat, at the same time examining its texture) "that life is an interwoven fabric." He paused a moment and added, "I got that puttin' of it from a book I've bin readin'."

We walked on, and he asked suddenly:

"Know anythin' about apples?"

"I believe they are reported to have affected the destiny of mankind," I answered. The postman smiled. He knew his Bible.

"The more I see o' these things," Ned continued (here he swept his arm round in a circle which embraced the green fields and everything that lived there), "the more I'm sartin that there is no such thing as independence. Nature is one big text preachin' that 'No man liveth unto hisself.'" He looked at me to see whether I was following him, so I nodded my encouragement.

"You know them trees o' mine that grow by the wall int' garden? They're Cox's pippins — grand stuff. Well, for three years I haven't had a solitary apple till this year."

"You had plenty of blossom too," I said.

"Aye; plenty," Ned continued; "that was the mystery on't. Couldn't mek out what were wrong. I pruned 'em and there were no yield. I washed 'em and gave 'em plenty o' manishment — still no fruit. I was fair beat."

"You have a fine crop this year," I said. "What's the secret?"

"Bees," he answered laconically, and with a delighted chuckle. "Until this year there's hardly bin a bee in the district. Isle o' Wight disease took the lot off, and the skips stood empty."

14

Then the old man let himself go in the fashion that always thrilled me.

"Them blossoms opened out each year. They filled up their little wells wi' nectar, and then floated out their scented invitations for the guests they hoped 'ud come to the feast. But they neither made light of it nor went their ways." (He shot a quick glance at me to see whether I caught his allusion.) "They simply weren't there to receive it — and the life dust that the bees carry on their backs and legs never reached those blossoms, and they shrivelled up."

"You mean —?" I asked.

"I mean that every blossom has a seed-child lyin' in its cradle o' petals, and that the heart o' the wee thing never starts to beat till the bee brings to it the — the — the —"

"Elixir of life," I suggested.

"That's it," Ned said enthusiastically; "that's where book larnin' comes in — the elixir o' life. Them trees o' mine could *exist* without the bees, but they couldn't *live* without 'em. There's a difference 'tween existin' and livin', you know. And that's a story of all life," he added.

"Ned, old chap," I said appreciatively, "you have the heart of a poet. Do you remember the fairy story of the Sleeping Beauty?"

"Aye," he said, "I reckon I do."

"Well, you have just given me another version of it," I said.

"Fairy stories," said he shyly, and with a far-away look in his eyes, "is the gossip of angels."

★ ★ ★

Later in the day Raq and I were alone. We were resting under the shade of an oak, listening to the chatter and laughter of the dryads and nymphs that hide in all crystal streams. In my mind lay the delightful vignette that the postman had etched. The dog was busy with a bone which a farmer's wife had thrown to him.

"Raq," I said solemnly, "I have something to say to thee."

The dog looked up, sensitive to the change of tone in my voice.

"In the first place," I continued sternly, "you were guilty of an indiscretion this morning — you chased a cat in the village."

The culprit blinked at me with apologetic eyes. He had caught the word "cat," and knew quite well that he had fallen from grace.

"In the second place," I continued, "you are now eating some succulent morsels that once adorned a noble beast — in other words, you are gnawing a bone." The latter word caused his tail to quiver, and he picked up his treasure and brought it to me.

"I am going to show you that the cat and the bone are interwoven with the fabric of your doggy life, and, in case you may doubt it, I may say that even the great Darwin himself agrees with me. This will in future keep you from chasing cats for ever."

The old sinner settled himself on his haunches, and, seeing that no greater punishment than a lecture was to be meted out to him, curled up his lips with an ingratiating smirk.

"Cats go down to the clover fields at night because they know they will find the field mice there. The field mice haunt the clover fields because they know they will find plenty of big bees there. The bees linger about the clover because they are looking for their food in the flowers' cups. The clover crop thus becomes fertilized by the bees' visits, and thus a good yield is assured."

I paused a moment as the attention of my audience was being transferred to the movements of a water-vole that was devouring the stem of a rush. I called him to attention and proceeded:

"If you kill cats, which are the enemies of the mice, then the mice will increase in numbers, which means that, as they increase, so more bees will be killed and eaten. Fewer bees means less fertilizing of the clover, which finally culminates in a poor crop. A poor crop of clover means that the cattle do not get the best of foodstuffs, and, therefore, Raq, my boy, poorly fed cattle means that you do not get good juicy bones."

By this time the dog was sound asleep, and his soft, snappy barks proclaimed that he was in the happy hunting-ground of dreams.

The interwoven fabric — cats, mice, bees, clover, cattle. An interlaced society — tinker, tailor, soldier, sailor. An interlinked community — capitalist, socialist, employer, employee — all touching and influencing and necessary to each other — fertilizing each other, and shrivelling under a forced independence.

Raq had fallen asleep in the midst of my facts. But, after all, he is only a dog.

The Farm

Of all the many recreations which I enjoy, I believe that "pottering about" holds first place in my affections. It is the art of loitering — not with intent to commit a felony, but in order to see the most in that small radius of territory which lies within a few yards of one's eyes. I feel I have a great deal in common with him who said, "The eyes of a fool are in the ends of the earth."

There are many such places which are favourites of mine. I delight to linger wherever there is the sound of running water. How can I do justice to the pleasure which is more akin to a spell which steals over me as I rest on some mossy bank listening to the breeze as it rustles the tops of a field of oats, barley, or wheat?

But, of all the places which lure me to stay, the farmyard has a supreme fascination.

To begin with, I love its varied smells and scents. Even those which are not usually associated with lavender or attar of roses give me a pleasure that I cannot describe. I look over the low walls of the sty, and what I should describe as offensive were it to greet me in the city I find a certain pleasure in now that I am in rural surroundings.

Of course, if the inhabitant be an old sow, and running round her be a litter of youngsters, then the

18

picture is complete. I wait for her to give a grunt of interrogation as she sees my face peering at her. I answer her politely, quietly, soothingly, and she at once imparts a slightly different tone to her next effort. It is less harsh, less suspicious. She accepts me as a well-wisher, and, all fears having departed, she rolls over on to her side. Immediately there is a rush amongst the young life that is ever hungry, to secure, so to speak, the best seats.

What a magnificent sight of anxious motherhood is it to see those rooting, pushful, vigorous piglets getting a morning meal! How careful is she lest her ponderous weight crush one of those silken-haired, pink delights! How they squeak out their woe and indignation until the warm stream of nutrition trickles down their outstretched throats, and until, at last, nothing can be heard save the mother's hard breathing and an occasional squeal of protest from some youngster whom another tries to displace!

Then at the end of the feeding crowd I look for the "runt" or the "reckling." It is the weakest of the lot. You can always spot him.

There he is, and he must take his chance with the strongest. His little legs are not so sturdy as those of his brothers and sisters — you can see his ribs pressing out from his spare body. He takes what is left after all the others have had their fill. Youth for him is going to be a struggle. Perhaps he will survive — perhaps not. But, with all her motherhood, there is no hint that the old sow has any particular sympathy for little "runt." If he lives, he lives.

But in human society it is the "reckling" to which we pay special attention. It is the "reckling" which survives and lives, perchance, to pass on its weakness to others, who may in their turn be "recklings" too. In Nature the weakest go to the wall. In human nature the weakest receive the strength of the strong — what a gulf really separates the two kingdoms!

I seat myself on the cobble-stones with my back to the barn wall, Raq by my side, just to see the variety entertainment that will pass before me. On their way to the pond, march a line of ducks. I can never see either a "Runner" or an "Aylesbury" without an inward chuckle of delight. They remind me somehow of "jovial monks with good capon lined." They are one of Nature's jokes, and, with ill-balanced bodies and short legs, waddle their way to the water. Strange, how unclean feeders such as ducks and pigs still provide the most tasty dishes!

I remind myself, as I watch them, that they are domesticated. The wild has been exorcized. That magnificent alertness of the mallard has been lost. They have bartered away their freedom, with its perils, for servitude, with its assured meals. They have even lost the power of flight, and have become egg-producers and an accessory to green peas. I find myself wondering what *I* have gained and lost — all due to the domestication of natural qualities. There is — But that is another story.

Over in the yard by the byre a dozen hens are chasing one which has found a crust. Stupid and selfish creatures! They will each in turn get the crust when the temporary owner puts it down before attempting to break it in pieces.

But just in front of me is a hen with chicks. She finds a seed, and all her instincts are to swallow it at once. But motherhood has transformed her into one of the most unselfish and tireless of guardians. A cluck rings out to her fluffy treasures. A cascade of buff beauties tumble round her beak, and the foremost one secures the prize.

Then Raq moves discontentedly, and immediately the hen swings round with feathers fluffed out and wings drooping, eyes ablaze, ready to do battle for those innocent "cheepers" she is trying to rear. Magnificent motherhood!

So I watch the interesting pageant before me, and whether it be the house-martins feeding their young, or the wagtail as it trips daintily round the margins of the pond — even though the hawk and stoat are part of their world, and a menacing part, too — yet I note the quiet confidence and freedom from care that pervades everything that lives.

In the midst of my musings I hear cheery voices. It is Alan and Joe, on whose farm I am.

"Come in and have a bit of something to eat — you'll be needing it." This is the summons to have what they call in Cumberland "The ten o'clock" and in Cheshire as "Baggin."

It is the half-way reviver between an early breakfast and a twelve o'clock dinner. In that peerless northern county you quaff large cupfuls of tea, but concentrate your energies on what is known as "plate cake." It is as delicious as manna, and has another point in common, viz. it won't keep. It is simply a bag of pastry, shaped like a plate, and stuffed with apples or blackcurrants. Be it noted that, in the best of these cakes, the fruit reaches from the centre to the extreme circumference. There is no wide parterre or margin of dry pastry.

In Cheshire you receive cheese and bread, not bread and cheese, and usually you have to hunt hard for the bread.

"What's your next job?" I ask Joe, hoping that I shall not be called upon to do too violent exercise before eleven o'clock.

"I'm going up to have a look at some sheep that are coughing a bit," he says.

"Far?" I query, thinking still of the manna.

"About half a mile or thereabouts," says Alan, leaving us for the plough.

I instantly multiply this by two. A townsman's mile and a countryman's are not quite the same measure.

And so we set out up the hill which holds heaven in its heart. "Had a good harvest?" I ask, as we pass the stacks.

"Fairish to middlin'," he answers guardedly. "Some we got in was all right in spite o' the rain. Wheat was quite good — it'll stand a bit o' weather, you know. Oats weren't quite so good. But I've seen worse — a good deal worse."

"You couldn't sing, then, 'All is safely gathered in'?" I continued.

"No, not exactly," said he, "but only short-sighted folks would boggle at it."

"Aye," I said, in a rising, trailing tone which was not an assent, but rather an invitation to proceed.

"There's such a lot o' harvests that you can be thankful for, even if hay and corn crops are none too good. There's the harvest of lambs and calves — there's the harvest of coal. They tell me that in Cornwall they have a harvest festival with their catches of fish."

"That is so," I said, "and look around you. Do you see that chestnut like burnished copper, and that dog-rose, scarlet with its berries? Do you see that stubble gleaming gold against that pearly sky, and the kestrel over yonder poised above the grass? That, my friend, is a little of the harvest of beauty — never failing, ever changing, free to all without money and without price."

We were on the stubble now, and in the corner of the field I noticed two or three sheaves still standing.

"What's the matter with those?" I asked.

"Just a fancy of mine," he said; "I leave the birds a pecking for when the hard weather comes."

I could see that he did not wish to say much about this "whim" of his, but I said by way of leading him on:

"We owe a big debt to the birds."

"That's just how I feel," he said. "I look upon 'em as hands that I don't have to pay. Those peewits over there do the land a terrible lot of good by ridding it of insects, and even the rooks" — he called them crows — "though they do a bit o' damage, root out the wire-worms. So I leave 'em a bit of something to go on with."

23

I should like to have pursued the subject, but our attention was attracted by Raq.

Before us, only a few yards ahead, a magnificent hare had sprung from her "form."

"Watch her!" I cried as the dog started on the chase. That is the worst of the best of spaniels. They have never learned the full art of restraint. All dogs are tempted to "rush in." In pointers and setters we have practically eradicated it.

We jumped on to a gate and laughed at the uneven race.

The hare soon had the measure of her assailant's pace, and took things very casually. Raq lumbered along like an old tank, his long ears flopping and flapping with every stride. He soon gave it up, and came back looking very foolish.

What did you do that for?" I asked severely. "Couldn't you see from the first jump that she was signalling to you that you hadn't an earthly chance of catching her?"

"What do you mean by that?" asked Joe.

"Why," said I, "that hare, as soon as she started to run, put her ears up. Those ears have black tips to them. That is one of the distinguishing marks of a hare. It is the first flag that she shows, and it says to any understanding creature of experience, 'Look at my ears! You are not chasing a common rabbit! I'm a sixty-mile-an-hour steeplechaser! Better save your wind and strength! You can only catch me when I'm napping, and that's not often'."

We climbed up to the top of the gate. The hare was seated two fields away, quietly combing out the fur which covers the bottom of her beautiful feet. She was in no way distressed or anxious.

"She's a timid creature and one of the most harmless that lives," I said, looking severely at Raq, who cringed at my tone and begged for mercy.

"Did I ever tell you what happened in that far spinney of yours?" I asked, turning to Joe. He shook his head.

"I was walking there in the spring and found a leveret — a tiny wee mite just a few days old. So I picked it up, and it squealed piteously."

"Nothing worse for squealing than a hare when it's hurt," said Joe.

"Then," I continued, "I heard a rustle in the bushes behind me, and, with eyes blazing with fury, ears up, and with a thudding noise made by her back feet, came a full-grown hare. She was the mother of the youngster I held. She reminded me of a cavalry charger coming full tilt at me. Then she turned and rushed away."

"Too timid to tackle you," said Joe.

"Probably; but the real wonder lies here. That brave little soul thought her youngster was squealing at the sight of a stoat. And, though she herself is terrified at the thought of a stoat, yet she was ready to face that terrible foe and risk her own life, if haply she might save her young one. Motherhood is a marvellous transformer."

"She found you too big a proposition to tackle, I reckon," said Joe.

"That's why she turned tail," I said.

We moved homewards after again looking at the distant hare and sending her a silent tribute of admiration. We did not talk very much. That is the best of Joe — he knows when to be quiet. He was thinking too. As we entered the house for dinner he looked at me and said quietly:

"That story of yourn set me thinking."

He said nothing more until we were sitting down at the table, when he whispered to me:

"Perfect love casteth out fear."

He looked at me, and, with the hare in my mind, I nodded comprehendingly.

Ownership

Raq and I had turned into a farmyard and were sitting with our backs against a stack which stood by itself.

Before us was the Dutch barn, with a substantial part of last year's hay still untouched.

I delight in idling in such a place. From the byre comes the sweet smell of cattle. Sometimes you can hear the steady crunching of the Clydesdales or Shires in their stables. How full of content is the sound!

By the side of the stacks the dainty wagtail runs with mincing steps, whilst the gallant cockerel, on finding some succulent morsel, calls to the hens which are committed to his care.

Yet, behind this surface peacefulness, fierce passions are soon roused, passions which are very much akin to those which sleep in us.

I believe it has been said that "animals are free from the mania of owning things." Like all general conclusions and sweeping assertions, such a statement is only partly true.

The dog by my side is as gentle a creature as one would wish to possess. Let any one else but me trifle with the bone which he is gnawing, and a deep warning growl will soon dispel this fallacy; the dog says, "This is mine, and what I hold I keep."

Sometimes this sense of ownership has its touch of comedy.

From the open door of the farmhouse a cat walked steadily, with a piece of meat in its mouth. It looked to the right and to the left, for a cat is notoriously suspicious.

Then, not seeing the dog and myself it came to a standstill under the shadow of the barn.

There it placed the piece of meat, which I thought had been stolen from the larder. Then, with that quiet precision which marks a cat's mode of eating, she drew herself together until she almost looked like a ball of black fur, and with meticulous care began to masticate the stolen food.

"You would have bolted it at once, old man," I thought, glancing at the dog by my side.

On looking across at the cat engrossed in her meal, I noticed a dark shadow fly down from the roof of the Dutch barn. It was a jackdaw, and with insolent swagger he walked in front of the cat, who ceased to eat and watched him with suspicious, baneful eyes.

Jack took good care to keep a safe distance, and simply contented himself with tantalizing his victim by strutting to and fro, causing her to revolve and face him in all his movements.

I could not at first make out what deep game the black bird was playing. I thought that he was going to be rash enough to make a dash for the piece of meat, which he evidently coveted.

After a moment or two of this harmless skirmishing the plot unfolded itself.

On the roof of the barn, but behind the cat, who was facing her tormentor, appeared a second daw.

Then, with great cleverness, the first bird feinted as though he were about to rush in on the cat. That she thought so too was evident from her preparation to give him a warm welcome.

Such tactics, however, for the moment, took all her attention.

Then, whilst she bristled with hate towards the first bird, there was a quick sweep down towards her by the newcomer.

Puss saw the shadow behind her or heard the rustle of wings, and, quick as thought, turned to receive the attacker in the rear.

That was the chance for which the first freebooter had been waiting. Like a flash he dashed in, and pounced on the prize which lay unguarded; and, before the cat could defend her own, he had seized it and, with a scream of triumph, vanished out of sight.

I could not help laughing at such a comedy, though in a sense I felt sorry for the cat. Yet those two wicked brainy pirates really deserved a reward for such a well-thought-out scheme, and one that had a good deal of hazard in it also.

After a rest, the dog and I went on to that part of the estate where we knew we should come across John Fell, the gamekeeper.

As we walked along I told him of the incident, and he said:

"Aye, them daws have a lot o' sense fer some things, but in others it's surprisin' how daft they be. That's one o' the surprising things i' Nature. Yer find traces o' deep schemin' in what might be called extraordinary things, and then yer come across the same birds doin' the stupidest things imaginable."

He drew me to the side of the hedge and pointed to an old castle in the distance.

"That's crowded with Jacks," he continued, "and if yer were to watch 'em buildin' their nests yer would soon see what I mean."

"They build in chimneys and the holes of buildings, don't they?" I asked.

John nodded, and said:

"I was watchin' a pair last 'ear as was buildin' in a sort o' chimney that was only about a foot wide."

He paused for a moment so that his words might impress me the more.

"Would you believe it," he continued, "those birds came with eighteen-inch twigs in their beaks — carried 'em crosswise, found they wouldn't go in that way, and so —" He looked at me to finish the sentence.

"They cocked them up on end and slid them into the hole," I answered.

John grinned.

"Not a bit of it," he said. "Them birds which you saw so cunnin' with the cat hadn't the sense fer that. They found the twigs wouldn't go in crosswise, so they dropped 'em on the ground and went away to seek fer more."

"However do you account for such stupidity," I asked, "especially in the face of the seeming wisdom they displayed in snatching the meat?"

"Hidebound by instinct," said John. "Fer thousands of years they've carried twigs in that way simply because it was their way o' doin' things. What intelligence they have was never called on."

"That reminds me somewhat of a hen I heard of," I said. "She was known by all on the farm as Emily."

"Go on," said John, "you can't tell me anything about a hen that's too stupid to have 'appened."

"Well," I continued, "Emily was a bit soft in the upper regions. She showed it by being in a continual state of broodiness. Whatever she came across, whether it was a potato or a brick, she settled down upon it and tried to hatch it out."

"She had a mother instinct," said John.

"Wait a moment," I said. "One day it occurred to the farmer that he would give the poor bird a chance. He was sorry for her — always 'sitting' and never hatching. So he gave her a real egg, which she mothered carefully in the usual way."

I paused — paused so long that John looked at me and said, "Well?"

"You finish off the yarn as I did yours," I said.

"Oh," said John readily enough, "she brought out the chick and became the proudest old bird in the farmyard."

It was my time to smile, and I answered him as he had answered me.

"Not a bit of it," I said. "As soon as she saw the live, squirming chicken come out of the egg, the shock was too much for her. She went clean off her head and rushed, demented, to the nearest pond, where she drowned herself."

"And how do ye account for that?"

"Instinct perverted and run to seed — untouched by intelligence, I should say," I replied. And I then added, "That's an American story!"

"Sounds like it!" John grunted, after which comment I could not get him to say another word on the subject.

As we walked along towards his house we passed a small orchard. The keeper halted and pointed to a couple of robins which were having a battle royal. Wings and beaks were working effectively in the struggle.

"Quarrelsome little beggars," I whispered to him; "fight even their own youngsters, don't they?"

"It's not merely quarrelsomeness," answered John; "there's more behind it than that. It's a case of providin' fer the race."

After a moment or two of watching the rivals he continued:

"Every robin has a keen sense of property owning."

I pricked up my ears, for this was the thought which had arisen in my mind as I watched the cat defend the meat.

"Robins," continued John, "feed largely on grubs, flies, insects, and worms — at least, this is the food they give to the young; and the feeding of the young is never long absent from their plans."

"All Nature lives for the race and not for the individual — eh?" I asked.

"That's about it," said the keeper. "Well, now," he continued, "in the mind of that robin is the pictur' of six or seven never-satisfied balls o' fluff, their mouths agape like the 'ever-open door'. Where's the food to come from? That's the problem."

He paused to watch one robin chase the defeated rival until the latter disappeared over the hedge at the bottom of the orchard. The little victor then flew back and surveyed us boldly from the branch of an apple-tree.

"It was that food-gettin' pictur'," said the keeper, "that caused the fight ye've just seen. Redbreast over there has decided to make this orchard o' mine his own private preserve — not because of its beauty, and not because he's got a miser's instinct. It's the larder for the new family that'll come along in the spring. Listen to t'other 'un now."

From beyond the hedge, over which the other contestant had disappeared, came the notes of a robin. Not the notes of song, but a harsh metallic, "Spik-spik."

The bird on the branch near to us turned at once in the direction of the call, and literally flung back a similar defiance at the challenger.

"That bird down there," said John, "hasn't had enough. There's plenty o' fight left in him, and I rather think he fancies this orchard fer hisself. He's tellin' this one near us that he'll live to fight another day."

"And what will be the end of it all?" I asked.

"The best man'll win and hold — t'other fellow will either find another bird and wrest his territory from 'im, or, failin' that, will have to find a place with vacant possession — some spot that nobody wants."

We turned into the cosy cottage of the keeper, and, whilst his daughter was preparing the tea, I noticed a ring flashing on the third finger of her left hand.

"Congratulations," I said, looking at the scintillating half-hoop.

She thanked me shyly and said, "I only got it yesterday."

"He's a decent sort o' chap," said John, looking affectionately at his daughter. "There'll be a job for ye, I reckon, next 'ear."

Whilst the cloth was being laid I turned and said to him:

"I've got a riddle for you. What's the connecting-link between that robin and Mary's ring?"

"Give it up," said John, after a moment or two.

"Well," said I, "the robin and the man act the same, but in different ways."

"Aye," said my companion, with a trace of indecision.

"The bird flings out his warning notes and patrols his territory, saying, 'This is mine — mine — mine'," I said.

John now saw what I was getting at, and slapped his knee delightedly.

"And," I continued, "the man slips on the half-hoop of diamonds which says to every one, 'This is mine — trespassers will be prosecuted: what I have I hold'. In both cases it is simply a matter of ownership."

WINTER

The Storing Instinct

I used to think that being the recipient of numerous invitations to "gatherings" and "parties" was a sign of popularity. Since we, as a small family, prepared a turkey for the Christmas festival, I am rather changing my ideas. The prospect of roast turkey is a delight. Its "finishing up" is a penalty. From Sunday to the following Saturday it returns to the table in various guises until at last the "twelve basketfuls" are emptied. But those who organize their festive gatherings insure against this dismal repetition, for the guests carry away with them that which becomes a tiresome menu.

There is one member of the family, however, who revels in the delights of the table. Never has he such a selection of bones to munch as at this season of the year. Of course, I refer to Raq. Even he, I have found, has his limits. Towards the end of the week I offered him a "drumstick." At ordinary times he would have seized it with avidity and have borne it in triumph to a selected corner. On this occasion, however, he took it reluctantly in his mouth, laid it on the floor for a moment, and then, seeing a look of displeasure on my face, picked it up and trotted through the kitchen door.

Behind the house there is what we call amongst our friends the "garden." It has in its midst a small grass plot — we refer to this as "the lawn" to those whom we are sure will never visit it. Around this "lawn" is a small strip of earth in which snapdragons and marigolds never do as well as groundsel, but where slugs, centipedes, and aphids enjoy themselves all through the summer season.

Raq crossed the grass, never looking to the right or left, and, finding a suitable position in the flower-bed, began to dig a hole, in which he deposited the bone and left it, buried.

As he was returning he caught sight of me, and, guessing that I had witnessed the whole incident — the desecration of the flower-bed — came crawling towards me with every sign of contrition.

"What have you been doing?" I asked severely.

Raq rolled over on his back, his tail wagging at a fearful rate, and I fancied that he said:

"I really do not know, master. I couldn't eat that bone. I'm absolutely full up and fed up with turkey, and I didn't know what to do with it. But, suddenly, something told me to bury it where I could find it again. So I went and did it. That's all."

I forgave the culprit, partly because he was so ingratiating, and also because of the thoughts he had raised.

Here was the "storing" instinct making itself manifest, though the need for it had disappeared. Raq was doing what his ancestors had learned to do thousands of years ago — prepare for the rainy day. After the feast and its repletion came days of scarcity, when the hunger moon looked down on a still cold world, when food became a problem and living dwindled to existence. Then it was that the dogs which had hidden secret stores of food managed to keep body and soul together. Those which had not shown such foresight laid themselves down, emaciated, weak, exhausted. The famished pack gave enfeebled members short shrift.

Raq was now in the land of plenty, but the old instinct had suddenly revived, and he had reacted to it.

Probably in that instinct lay all the modern ideas of cold storage. Probably, too, from the burying habit finally blossomed the building of a larder.

It is always well to have some main idea running through the mind, especially if one is having a tramp across country. The idea is like a snowball — it gathers as it rolls on; and, as Raq and I crunched our way through the white-covered fields, I kept returning to the morning's incident.

Outside the village, we came across one whom I knew as Jerry. He was a sort of handy-man to the farmers of the district and could do almost anything except regular work. How he lived was a mystery; he was a good-natured, cheerful idler, and, in spite of his haphazard ways, was a general favourite.

On his back was a bunch of curious wire contraptions, every one of which possessed a small wooden barrel.

"And what are you toiling at so hard to-day, Jerry?" was my greeting to him.

39

"I'm wastin' away, sir," said the old rogue, "at mole catchin'."

"Had any luck?" I asked.

"Only one; the weather's too hard, and when frost strikes deep, then the moles run deeper than I can set my traps," said Jerry.

He plunged his hand into a capacious pocket which lay inside his coat, and drew out the unfortunate mole.

"That's a fine pocket for keeping letters in," I said. "You must have a lot of correspondence."

Jerry grinned. "It'll hold a hare," he said, showing me its size, "and if ever you want one" — here he winked wickedly — "I know the sound that'll entice 'em here."

I took the mole from him and began examining it. To look at, it was as uncomely a thing as you will find. The front feet were sizes too large for its tubular-shaped body. They were hard and horny, and reminded me of the hands of a navvy. They were set, too, at a curious angle, the palms being turned outwards. They were perfect animal spades. Two small slits, which I suppose were meant for eyes, were set in a snout which reminded me of a cross between the nose of a hedgehog and that of a shrew.

Jerry watched me examining it, and then said:

"See any difference between its fur and the coat of a rabbit or a rat?"

Now, to tell the truth, I had noticed its wonderful pile, but I wanted to give my companion a chance to open out, so I shook my head.

"Well, feel this," he said, drawing out from his left-hand pocket a rabbit.

I held the rabbit in my hand. It was neither riddled with shot nor were a stoat's teeth-marks in the light fawn fur at the base of the ears.

"Never mind how it was killed," said the old rascal, as I pointed to a thin line plainly noticeable round the rabbit's neck. "Feel its fur — see how it lies flat, running from head to tail."

I carried out his directions.

"Now," he continued, "run your hand from the tail to the ears, and you'll feel that you are movin' against the grain."

He took the dead mole in his hands and worked his finger up and down its back.

"Try it," he said, handing it to me, "and see how different it is to that rabbit's. It runs either way. Then ask yourself 'Why?' There's a reason for everythin' in Natur'."

I did as I was commanded, and expressed my wonder.

"That's because he makes his tunnel so as to fit his body like a glove fits a hand. If he had fur like that 'un" — here Jerry pointed to the rabbit — "he'd never be able to move back'ards — the fur would catch in the top and sides of his burrow. But it stands straight up and bends to the right or left as easy as a willow wand. There's no defiance in that coat; it's all compliance."

"And how does he live in this cold weather?" I asked.

"Chases the worms, and the deeper they go to get away from the cold the deeper he drives his galleries," said my companion. "He's a regular miner, he is."

"He doesn't snare them with brass wire, then?" I said, looking meaningly at the rabbit.

The old poacher smiled. "I'll tell you somethin' that he does do. He lays up stores o' worms that he can find when he's hungry, and he's nearly always that. He's the biggest eater for his size that I know of. If he doesn't get a full meal every few hours he dies o' starvation."

"Lays up stores?" I asked incredulously. "How in the world does he lay up a store of worms? In hot weather they won't keep, and in cold they shrivel up —"

"He lays up a store o' live worms, I tell you," said Jerry decisively, putting the accent on the adjective.

I laughed at such a suggestion. "You're pulling my leg, Jerry," I said. "Why, they'd wriggle away in a few minutes, even if he managed to make a pile of them."

But Jerry was in deadly earnest, and, seeing that I doubted his word, decided to convince me by other arguments. This was typical of Jerry; if he couldn't land his fish with a net, he would try a gaff.

"You're a fisherman, aren't you?" he asked, and, not waiting for an answer, said: "Ever cut an eel's head off when he'd gorged the hook?"

I nodded, and he asked:

"What happened?"

"The gills went on moving naturally in the water for an hour or more," I answered, "and the rest of the body continued to wriggle for half a day as though it were alive."

"I've seen 'em squirm in the fryin'-pan," said Jerry, "after I've cut 'em up into little bits, and," he added triumphantly, "that's how the mole serves the worms. He bites their heads off, and the rest of 'em lives for hours. They can't wriggle away 'cos their nose is gone. They don't go bad and they don't shrivel up, 'cos they're partly alive. He stacks 'em up at the end of a tunnel, knowing well that, in a few hours, he may need 'em — that's the 'storing' instinct, and no mistake."

I looked at the dead mole with renewed interest. What a little chip of existence it looked when compared with Raq. But that little delver in the dark had gone one better than the dog. The latter knew how to store inert things, but this furry wonder actually managed to keep a live larder. Was that merely instinct without reason, or was there a mind which schemed and thought things out, which not only had an intense present, but also felt that there was such a thing as the future?

As we plodded along the roads we passed the farm. The cows were being turned out to get their afternoon drink. Seeing them gave me an idea.

"Ever studied the ways of ants?" I asked of my companion.

"No," he said, "only when I've sat too close to their nest. That makes you study how to get rid of 'em."

"Well," I continued, "I don't know a great deal about them myself, but I do know that they keep cows."

"Alan," shouted Jerry, catching sight of our mutual friend as he emerged from the byre. "What's the name of that feller in the Bible that died sudden-like through not speakin' the truth?"

"Ananias," promptly answered the farmer.

"Aye, that's him," said Jerry, as Alan joined us and looked questioningly at the speaker. "I just wanted to refresh my memory, that's all."

Then, seeing that I was really serious, he became silent, and, after explaining to the new-comer what had caused the question, I proceeded.

"You know the little green insects that settle on rose-trees?" Both men nodded.

"Well," I said, "they have the power of turning the sap they drink into a sugary syrup, and the ants are very fond of this sweet liquor."

"I've heerd o' that," said Jerry, in such a tone that he meant it to be an apology for his former incredulity.

"These green flies can either withhold or produce this drop of distilled sugar."

"A cow can hold back its milk if it likes," interpolated Alan.

"And the ants," I continued, "sometimes keep these aphids, as they are called, and by stroking and tickling them induce them to yield what to them is the nectar of the gods."

"It is said," I went on, "that the ants actually carry these green herds into their subterranean galleries, so that their handy and daily supplies can be obtained without the necessity of foraging."

"Wonderful," said Jerry.

"So you see, my friend," I said, turning to him, "Raq has learnt the art of storing dead things. The mole knows how to reserve the semi-alive. But the insect seems to possess the best brains of the lot, for it stores up for itself living fountains."

As I bade them good-bye, I turned to Jerry and said:

"You asked Alan just now for something out of the Bible. Here's something else that bears on our talk: 'Lay not up for yourselves treasures upon earth, where moth and rust doth corrupt, and where thieves break through and steal — but lay up for yourselves treasures in heaven'. That's the real 'storing' instinct."

A Shepherd of the Hills

It is a vexed question as to where the garden in which our first parents walked was situated. Some have placed it in Africa, others in Asia Minor.

I am not pretending to settle the point at issue. All I know is that there is a certain county in the North of England through which the River Eden winds its way, and for me, at all events, there is Paradise itself.

It was again my joy to tramp amidst its solitudes. I stood on its undulating, thawing fields, and, from the crest of one of them, gazed over miles of country which could produce all the sylvan delights of Devon, the suave beauty of Surrey, the ruggedness of the Highlands, and the pastoral dignity of Shropshire.

Far away in blue mist stood Helvellyn and Saddleback. But the Lake District, beautiful as it is, is not for me. It has become a "professional beauty." No part of it is sacrosanct. The "charas" have invaded its serene ghylls, and trippers sully its loveliness with untidy litter.

My choice lies in its untrodden ways, and those ways usually lead me on to the Fells.

I look up at them and see their curved summits. Once, in the dim past, they were jagged and their pinnacles split the sky. But frost, rain, and wind, those patient and persistent architects, have moulded them into serenity and quietness of contour. Compared with them in the matter of age, other pointed and irregular heights are upstarts — they are but of yesterday.

In the bosom of the Fells is locked the experience of the ages. There is no fussiness about them; neither is there fear. The future holds no terrors, for they know the past. Serene, majestic, undismayed they stand.

It was a wintry morning, but the fields were freed from the snow. All living things were actively searching for the food which, for many days, had been buried.

The rooks were driving their pickaxe-like bills into the softening earth. Every hedge-bottom had its searching birds, whilst flocks of finches and starlings rejoiced on the yellow stubble.

How frosty was the air, and yet how warm and comfortable the Fells looked at their bases.

The heights above were still crowned with snow. Every wrinkle on their rounded summits was limned in white.

But the track, a sheep's track, on which I walked, was framed in chestnut bracken, and great patches of amber grass rustled on the hill-side.

Far up on the hill-side I heard a whistle, and after some vigorous climbing, I met a shepherd. He was clad in grey tweed, while around his throat was thrown a red muffler. Baggy trousers, grey beard, blue eyes, which he had a habit of contracting, old brown cap, an ash stick cut from the hedge, completes his description. A lanky black-and-white collie dog lay at his feet.

After a few opening remarks, in which he sized me up and evidently thought I was one to be trusted and also of average intelligence, I began to lead him on to topics in which I was interested.

"It looks as though we were going to have a few days of fine weather," I said, looking up at the blue patches overhead.

"Mebbe," answered the shepherd, and, I thought, rather dubiously.

"You don't think so?" I asked. "How's the 'glass' this morning, rising or falling?"

"I've never set eyes on a glass fer months," he said, "but I reckon we shall have rain afore long — the auld wife was showin' hersel' as I left the hoose this morning."

"The auld wife was showin' hersel'" — the phrase puzzled me for a moment. Then it dawned on me that he was referring to those old-fashioned barometers. They represent a small Swiss chalet with two open doors. Two figures — an old man and an old woman — move in and out and foretell "rain or fine".

"I always thought that it was the old man who foretold bad weather," I said.

"Is't likely?" he answered. "It's allus the womenfolk who mak's the squalls. There are other signs too, I reckon."

I waited, without making any comment. If he were in the mood I knew that he would give reasons for his prophecy.

"Sheep seem to be uneasy-like this mornin', and there's one old tup [ram] up there" — here he pointed with his stick towards the summit — "allus tells ye what to expeck from the weather." He paused and scanned the distant heights. "Aye, there he is, look ye — it'll rain right enough."

I looked in the direction he pointed, and saw what to me was a horned sheep feeding with others of its kind. But I could see no connection between the old tup and the weather. I turned to my companion, and found him smiling at me — probably pitying the poor townsman who needed a barometer as a weather-prophet.

"See owt?" he said.

"Nowt," I answered, whereat the old boy laughed. The "nowt" put him in a good humour, and he began to throw off his reserve.

"That old tup," he said, "allus feeds with his tail to the wind when rain be comin' on. When he's head on to it, ye can expeck fairish weather. He never fails."

I looked up with renewed interest towards the heights. The tup was certainly feeding with his tail towards the wind.

"I suppose you never hear the wireless or listen to the weather forecasts, do you?" I asked.

"Verra seldom," he said. "I have heerd it, but I didna like it. Did ye see many rabbits oot feedin' as ye cam' along?"

I nodded, and said, "Scores of them."

"There ye are," he said, rubbing his rough hands together. "They're night-feeders, but if rain's comin' in the night, they know it — and they tak' their chance while it's dry-like. Aye," he added, "there'll be rain to-night."

We walked along together in silence, and, coming to a place which overlooked a wide stretch of country, the shepherd said, pointing to a grass field:

"There's anither sign fer ye."

I looked at the field to which his stick directed me. A number of rooks were busy on its surface.

"D'ye see yon wood behind 'em?" he asked. "That's their roosting-place. Not verra far away from it, are they? In fine weather they go miles away to find food. But not if they're likely to be caught in a storm. Aye, it'll rain all night, and heavy too," he added.

I put these weather-signs in my mental pocket-book. As I wrote them down with the pen of thought, I caught sight of others which I had picked up in my wanderings:

"When the scarlet pimpernel is closed, take your mackintosh."

"When the swallows hawk high in the air, then never fear the weather."

"When bees stay in the hive, don't go far away from a refuge."

"Rain before seven, fine before eleven."

"Mackerel sky — twelve hours dry."

I tramped on with the shepherd until we stood on a vantage-point which commanded a wide vista of hill and glen.

A sweep of his arm was all that was necessary to send the dog away on his errand of massing together the whole flock.

A moment before, the sheep had been quietly grazing. As soon as that lithe figure began to circle round them they threw up their heads, turned to face him, though he were far distant from them, and watched him as he made the wide circuit of the hills.

The shepherd gave a long, piercing whistle. The dog stood still for a moment, and, in response to the shrill command, climbed wider and higher.

"There may be a lone sheep aboot yon crag," said his master by way of explanation.

The next moment I saw that the shepherd had been correct. The dog was bringing down, not one, but three of them. They were descending at rather a reckless pace, and two staccato whistles made the dog pause, and his charges proceeded at a more leisurely pace.

As the flock came within earshot, my companion ceased to whistle, and I heard him shout, "Farther awa'", "Steady, lass, steady", and so on. Soon, standing in a compact quivering mass, the sheep, which a few moments before were dotting the landscape like little white sails, stood before us as a well-ordered company, their black-and-white drill-sergeant, with his tongue lolling out, ceaselessly but quietly patrolling their flanks.

"What breed are they?" I asked.

"That yin there," said he, pointing to one with a black face with white markings, "is a Swaledale; that yin with a black face comes fra' Scotland; and that grey-face yin is a crossbred — got with a Leicester tup and a black-faced yin."

"On the small side, aren't they," I said, thinking of the large South Down sheep I had seen.

"People wants small joints nowadays,' said my companion. "In my younger days they wanted a leg aboot seven or eight poonds in weight; now they're after the four-poonders. The black-faced are just right fer 'em."

After inspecting them and seeing that all was well, we turned to retrace our steps. The hills on which we were walking had neither walls nor hedges.

"How do you keep your sheep within bounds?" I asked. "What is to prevent them roaming down to the valley farms or wandering on to the land of another landlord?"

"I reckon they keep within bounds themselves," answered the shepherd.

Then he told me how these "silly sheep," as we call them, have an instinct for their own heath. Even were walls or dykes present on the Fells, they would not prevent these "mountaineers" from wandering. The check is in their own minds. They are perfectly free to roam. Their only limitation is the leash of their own desires.

As I left the shepherd making his way to his hut, I looked at the time. It was after three o'clock, and I had promised to meet my wife at two-thirty, and go down to the village.

I hurried down to the farm, and as the Parish Church boomed out the hour of four I came in sight of my destination.

Even from afar I could see a figure waiting by the door which opened on the spacious kitchen.

I redoubled my speed, but the words of the shepherd rang ominously in my ears: "When the auld wife's showin' hersel', then ye may look oot fer squally weather." The shepherd, I may add, proved to be no false prophet!

A Yuletide Decoration

It was a beautiful morning, and Nature had decided to give the world a real Christmas covering. Snow had fallen during the night, and when the fields lie under their white counterpane, then is the time to learn what the wild folk have been doing. For a few hours a newspaper of their secluded lives is spread for all to read, and, wherever they have moved, they leave behind them a record of their wanderings.

Here is a rabbit warren, and around it is a bewildering network of footprints. The tracks clearly point to the fact that these little creatures have been perplexed at finding all their feeding-places hidden by the snow. Some of the knowing ones have scratched until they found a little verdure. Most of them, however, went back to their dark corridors as empty as when they left them. They had never seen snow before.

By the wood are the broad three-toed marks of the lordly cock-pheasant, and where his tail trailed on the ground has been faithfully registered by the glistening whiteness.

In the centre of the stubble-field is a dark, circular patch. On examination it proves to be a circle where the snow has been thawed. Here, a covey of partridges has spent the night, tail to tail, heads turned outwards and forming the circumference of the pack. What disturbed them, and why they fled with a great whirring of wings, may be seen by the far hedge. There lie footprints, compact as a cat's, and giving the impression that they had been made by a one-legged creature. They are the tracks of a fox, and he had looked greedily at the birds, which he had scented a score of yards away. Happily for them, their sentinel had not slept, otherwise there might have been a few chestnut feathers blowing over the field, and perchance a few red drops staining the virgin whiteness that covered all things.

Nearly all living things are at a loss what to do when snow falls. Even Raq, as he trotted along, showed unusual listlessness. There was no scent left behind of any living thing, and a spaniel without a scent is as useless as a hawk without eyes. He brightened up, however, as the village came into view. Here he knew that he would come into his own again, even though we only explored the byres and barns.

And so we walked down the quaint village street, and, as we journeyed on, faces appeared at windows and doors, and voices flung me a nosegay of the season's compliments.

"Come in; have a bite o' summat," said one of the many hospitable souls, and, knowing that sooner or later I should have to capitulate to their importunities, I entered the cottage of Sally Stordy.

"Fancy bein' out in sic' weather," said my hostess, and when I told her how I enjoyed it she added, "Well, every man to his taste."

Soon I was seated before a table on which lay a couple of smoking rashers. Raq was contenting himself with a bone.

"You remember Sarah Ann?" asked my benefactress.

"When did she die?" I asked guardedly, not being able to recall the owner of the name, and judging by the tone of the questioner that something tragic had occurred.

"We killed her — that's 'er ye're eatin'," said my friend, taking off her apron.

For a moment I had an inward sinking sensation. Then, with infinite relief, it dawned on me that Sarah Ann was the name of their sow, and one which I had often admired.

"She were a right good 'un, she were," said she, with a sigh.

"She is," said I, interring pieces of Sarah with relish.

"We shall never see 'er likes agen," the good soul said regretfully.

"Never again," I murmured, as I finished my repast, and, in spite of its flavour, feeling that somehow or other I had been present at a memorial service.

"Here's a slice or two for your missus," she said, handing me a good-sized parcel, "and here is a bottle of 'cleat' wine. Made it myself. No need to be afeard on it. It's teetotal."

And so, fortified within and without, we went out into the snowy roads. What splendid, unspoilt souls these country folk are! Silver and gold have they none, but such as they have, give they unto you.

We called at the home of Ned, the postman, and, finding that he was going to a neighbouring village, we set off with him.

When we were leaving the last of the houses behind us, I turned to him with my stock question:

"And what have you been thinking out lately?" He was about to answer when a troop of boys and girls came round the bend of the road, two of the boys bearing big armfuls of holly.

"And what have ye been up to now, you young rascals?" asked Ned of the uproarious group.

"Getting 'olly for the school — to 'ang it up," said one of the boys.

"Aye," said the old man, "I see you have." Then he paused a moment and continued: "And you got that bunch, Dick Thompson, from pretty near the ground; and yours, Jimmy Dale, had to be climbed for."

"Yer right, Ned," said the boy Dick, with a tone of admiration in his voice. "Jimmy had to get up a rowan-tree to reach the lump he has. Tell us, how did you know that?"

The old postman smiled and shook his head. "Not now; haven't time to stop and talk to ye. Ask me another time and I'll tell ye."

And so we passed on, and I knew that within the next few days Ned would be seated on a favourite stone with his back to a barn, and round him would be grouped a bunch of inquiring and interested youngsters.

I determined to press the question which Dickie Thompson had asked.

"But how did you know from what parts of the tree the holly had come? It looked pretty much all the same to me."

For a moment or two Ned made no reply. Then he turned towards me and said:

"You believe in disarmament and the League o' Nations, don't ye?"

"I do," I answered heartily.

"Well, the holly-tree, if you study it at all, will give you a few points which you can think about. Have you ever thought that this world" — here he raised his arm and swept fields, dales, rivers, hedges, woods into his embracing thought — "have you ever thought that all of it lives, so to speak, on a war footin'?"

"Well," I said, "I have in my own mind divided all animals into the hunters and the hunted."

"Aye," said he, "that's all right. But even the plants, shrubs, and trees must be included. Ye must not only think of the stoat after the rabbit, and the kestrel after the mouse, but you must think of the cattle as bein' the enemies of everything that grows. Do you think the hedges want to be eaten?"

"I hadn't thought of it in that light," I answered.

"Ah," said the postman, with a chuckle, "but many of the trees 'as, and they've met the danger with foresight and cunning. Well, now, take the holly as a sample. Here is a tree which knows that when winter comes round it'll be one of the only green things left standing in the fields. Around it'll be nothin' but stripped hedges and tasteless, sodden grass. It knows, too, that every cow or horse that's longing fer a taste of some green thing will single it out fer special attention. So its chances of escape are precious few."

He looked at me to see whether I was following his statements.

"I follow you, Ned," I said, and I added, "Of course, the real trouble of the tree is that it cannot take refuge in flight. It is tethered to one place."

"That's it, exactly," said my companion. "Well, then," he went on, "just as the nettle has its stinging-needles, so the holly-tree has turned itself into a kind of green hedgehog, and nothing with a tender, sensitive nose ever thinks it worth while to tackle it."

We trudged on in silence for a few minutes, and, thinking that the old man had finished, I said:

"But that doesn't explain how you knew from what part of the tree the youngsters had cut their bunches."

"I'm coming to that," he said abruptly, so abruptly that I felt for a moment that I myself was attempting to browse on a holly-bush. I had forgotten that he did not like to be interrupted save when he invited it.

"Now, every bush knows that it can't do two things successfully. If it grows prickles — defences — it can't put all its strength into its leaves or fruit. If ye 'ave yer armaments, something must suffer. If ye spend five million pounds on a battleship, ye can't have it fer eddication."

He paused, and I saw by his look that at that moment I was expected to say something.

"I've been reading quite lately that cattle experts say that experiments go to prove that hornless cattle make more beef and better quality than horned ones. They say that the growing of horns is an appreciable drain on the beast's strength. No horns means better and more meat."

"Mebbe that is so," said Ned, "though I'm not fond of 'cush' cows myself. Howsomever, the holly-tree acts as though it knew this; and now comes the answer to them boys and girls. The leaves of the tree which are nearest to the ground and just where their danger of bein' eaten is the greatest, have the most prickles on. But, when you look at the branches above seven or eight feet high, you find that the defensive points are not so numerous — in fact, in some holly-bushes they aren't to be found at all. So you can see how easy it was fer me to tell them childer where their bunches grew. Dickie Thompson's lot was nearly as prickly as a gorse-bush; so he had to do no climbing to get it. Jimmy Dale's had more berries on and less spines; so he had harder work to get his'n."

We left Ned to do his business in the village, and Raq and I branched off into open country.

Ned's explanations about the holly had certainly been intriguing. I could not help wondering whether the bush had developed spines in order to defend itself from its enemies, or whether, somehow or other, those prickles had come into existence in the ordinary course of development. Then the natural result would be for all "browsers" to avoid it. Could the plant think out a plan of campaign such as Ned had hinted at?

And yet Sir Jagadis Chandra Bose, the Indian botanist, who has specialized on plant life, tells some uncanny facts concerning the *mind* of the plant. He has registered its heart-beats, stayed its death by poisoning, and has witnessed its response to stimulants.

I thought of the pine-tree and its exuding resin; the latter takes the place of our bandages for a wound. When the tree is cut, the gum covers the gash and wards off damaging bacteria. Chance?

I mentally inhaled the scent of varied plants due to the manufacture of certain volatile oils. They attract the insects that are necessary to fertilization, yet are fatal to bacteria — fascinator and sanitizer in one. Chance? The rhododendron is green during the winter, but plates itself with silica, so that anything that swallows it suffers from internal pains and avoids it ever afterwards. Are all such wonders due to something more or less fortuitous, or is there a glimmer of intelligence behind it?

Be that as it may, life for them is a struggle, and out of the struggle issues vitality, inventiveness, patience, persistence.

Plovers' Eggs

Sometimes, when my time is limited, I am obliged to give the farm itself a wide berth. That is because both Hannah and Charlotte, the sisters of Joe and Alan, will insist that I have "a bite o' summat" at whatever hour I appear. It is the kindness of forcible feeding.

Consequently Raq and I pushed on towards the High Barn. This is the outpost of the farm, and, as the name indicates, it stands on the summit of a hill.

When I think of solitude, my mind ever turns towards "the Hee Barn," as Alan calls it. For many months in the year it gazes on the Fells, where every gully is lined with snow. Before it lies a valley where crystal streams for ever glide, and where homesteads seem to have grown naturally rather than to have been built.

The barn is a landmark for the whole district. When the mists veil its grey walls, then those below look out for squalls and stormy weather. The birds, too, as they wing their way, give it welcome and greeting. The wild geese salute it as they head for the estuary, and the "Honk, Honk," of the leader announces to his followers that another signpost has been passed.

It was here that I found Joe and Alan. They gave us a quiet but sincere welcome that showed itself in tone rather than in a multiplicity of words. Raq also gave them his "best selected" affection.

They were seated in the barn having their "ten o'clock," which, as North countrymen know, is a specially ordained "snack" in the middle of the morning to prevent outdoor workers from undergoing the perils of starvation. Just a plain meal, but, when the condiment is the fragrance of last year's hay, what more can one ask for?

"And what has been your job this morning?" I asked, turning to Alan.

"We've bin sowin' oats," he answered. "Rather late, you know, but weather's bin so bad we couldn't get on to the fields."

"Seen any plovers' eggs?" I asked.

"Aye," Alan answered, "quite a few. But, of course, we've smashed a few — couldn't help it. I'm fond o' them birds, and like to see 'em on the land all through the winter."

I shook my head, and Joe asked:

"What are ye shakkin' yer head about?"

"Well," I said, "you may have seen a few plovers in your fields all through the winter months, but these birds that are nesting now are not the winterers."

"No?" said Alan, in a tone that indicated he was too polite to contradict me, but that he was unconvinced.

"Those birds which wintered here," I continued, "were migrants from the cold North. But they have left

63

again now that the snows have cleared. Those that are nesting here now migrated in the autumn to the South of England and the North of France. Bird-life is like the sea; it ebbs and flows."

"They've a queer taste wantin' to come here in the winter," said Joe.

"One man's poison is another man's meat," said Alan philosophically. "When we say 'It's gey cold to-day', them northern tuwhits'll be noddin' to each other and sayin', 'What nice weather we're havin''."

"Have you noticed anything very interesting about the plovers' eggs?" I asked.

"Can't say as I have," answered Alan, "save that when the full clutch is laid, you allus find 'em with their pointed ends turned towards the centre o' the nest. I've often picked 'em up and left 'em lyin' anyhow in the nest. But when I passed it agen the eggs had allus bin neatly arranged."

"Let us go over to the field," I said.

So we all of us walked to where the birds had elected to make their nursery.

No sooner were we there than several couples rose in the air. "Peet-a-weet, a weet," they cried, swerving, diving, swooping, volplaning in their excitement. In the next field one was making a peculiar buzzing with its wings.

"Hear that?" I asked.

"You only hear that in early spring," said Alan. "What is it?"

By way of answer I looked sideways at Joe, and said to Alan:

"How did Joe get himself up when he was courting Sally? Did he go to see her in the clothes he's wearing now?"

"He looked a reg'lar swell," answered Alan, with a grin. "Used to oil his hair and put on socks and ties that made every horse in the neighbourhood shy wi' fright. And his cap —"

"Enough!" I cried, seeing that Joe was preparing to take strong measures; and, pointing to the plover, I said:

"That bird is just acting like us human beings. He is presenting himself to his mate in the best possible light."

"Showin' off his points," said Alan.

"Exactly," I answered. "When we want to make an impression on any one, we put on our most becoming clothes, try to look smarter than any rival. Even so does the plover. Look at the crest he erects on the top of his head. Notice the metallic sheen of his darker feathers, the ivory whiteness of his underfeathers. And to call attention to his aerial agility, and to make his mate feel what a fine companion she has chosen, he makes the noise with his wings that you can now hear."

For a moment or two we stood and watched the antics of the bird.

"I think also," I said, "that it uses the sound to frighten off intruders from land which it considers to be its preserve."

After a few minutes' search we came across the nest for which we were searching.

"There you are," said Alan, "the eggs are pointing inwards, as I told you they would be."

For a moment or two we looked down at them. What a wonder of colouring, what a marvel of mimicry! They toned so well with their surroundings that if you looked away for a moment, you had to scrutinize the ground very carefully before your eyes "picked them up" again.

"Have you a piece of wire?" I asked.

Both of my companions searched in their pockets, and, finding none, began to explore the possibilities of the hedge.

Finally, Joe brought me a piece, and I twisted it into a circle, which, when placed on the nest, just encircled the four eggs.

"Pick it up carefully," I said to Alan, and, a moment later, I turned the four eggs so that their rounded ends all turned towards the centre.

"Now," I continued, "put the wire ring back again and notice the difference."

Alan did as I bade him; but the ring no longer enclosed the eggs. It lay on top of them, and outside of the chaplet the four points of the eggs protruded.

"Clever bird," said Alan, bending low over the nest. "Knows how to save space, and knows the best position to put 'em in so that she can keep 'em warm."

"She knows more'n that," said Joe, who has a good working knowledge of ordinary engineering, and who had picked an egg up and was examining it carefully.

"See the point on it?" he asked, looking at his brother. "Well," he added, "it gives the egg a streamline body."

Alan took the egg and said:

"I'm not sure that I know what you mean."

For answer, Joe selected a piece of ground, and, with the aid of a stone, levelled and rolled it flat.

"Put the egg down here," he said.

Alan did so, and was commanded by his brother to stoop down and blow hard at it.

"Notice anything?" Joe asked.

"Aye, I did," said Alan; "it turned round in a circle. A hen's egg would have rolled off that flat land."

"So would a plover's roll out of its small nest if it hadn't that pointed end," said Joe. "When there's only one egg in it and the wind blows hard —"

"Aye, and it can blow, too, up here," said Alan, turning to me for a moment.

"Then," continued his brother, "this little egg, instead of being blown about like a cork, slews round and faces the wind with its thin end. That's what I mean by having a streamline body."

As we walked back again down the hill, Alan said:

"These birds and their eggs are protected now, and so they ought to be. The plover is the farmer's friend."

"Do you know the biggest foe these lapwings ever had?" I asked.

"Go on," said Joe.

"The Covenanters of Scotland," I continued. "Every clutch of eggs they found was ruthlessly destroyed — and for a good reason. No warier bird lives than this

67

crested migrant. No bird, man, or beast enters a brooding plover's domain without the plaintive cry of this watcher filling the air. No Covenanter, hiding from the searching soldiery, was safe in his hiding-place whilst this bird hatched her eggs near to him. Every time he moved, she rose and cried forth to the world, 'There's a man about'. Hence, in his extremity, the Covenanter destroyed them."

And so, with the lapwing's querulous notes still in our ears, we parted. Alan went back to his horses and the harrow. Joe went on to the lambs.

As I walked homewards I tried to recall a story that I had heard concerning plovers' eggs. For some time I could not lift it out of the depths of memory. Even now I do not think I have all its details, but originally I believe it was told by J. E. Buckrose in a delightful essay "On Giving".

There was an old couple, man and wife, who were extremely fond of each other, but never showed it very much outwardly. It was the custom of the old man — and had been for forty years or more — to take a walk round a certain mere, once every spring-time, in order to find a few plovers' eggs.

These he brought home for his wife's tea. He never gave her any other present, because it was all they could do to live. But every year he used to bring that one offering, and watched her as she ate them, always making the same remark, "You've gotten your eggs, Maria, so we shall soon have the roses out on the porch, now summer's comin'."

Then he died. The neighbour, however, was a kindly soul, so, next spring, she persuaded her husband to walk round the fields and find a few plovers' eggs for old Mrs. Brown.

Then, carrying them in her hands, she took them into the cottage, with her pleasant face all smiles.

"Look, here's your eggs all the same. Now sit you to the table and enjoy them." But the old woman turned her head aside.

"Take 'em away," she said; "I can't abide 'em. I never could."

"You never could? But your husband —" began the young woman, astounded.

Then her eyes met those other sunken ones, and she became silent, for she too loved her man very dearly, and so she understood.

SPRING

The Touch of Spring

I dare not say that the "Winter is over and gone," because one never knows what will happen in this country. But when I was out with Raq the other morning, I felt that I could positively say, "Spring is near at hand".

We sat down together, not because I was tired, but because I like to give my senses a chance of enjoying themselves.

Sometimes I allow my sense of smell a monopoly right of enriching itself. At other times my eyes get the privilege, to the exclusion of all other competing receiving-stations.

On this morning I put on one side the coils with which I "get" fragrances and "sights", and for a moment or two replaced them with those which ensnare the sounds of meadow and hill.

Above me in an elm was a young thrush — a cock-bird that had emerged from his green shell in the previous year. He had perched on the tree, and, somehow or other, the sunshine had loosened his vocal chords. Perchance, too, some warm fire had kindled behind his striped breast — a fire which we humans call "love"; and the sparks of that fire travelled upwards and fell out of his bill as song.

How he learnt his song I cannot say. Perhaps some dim memory revived notes which he had heard his father produce as he lay snug in the nest. Or, perchance, he may have been born with a kind of gramophone record stored within him, but which needed a certain outside stimulus to pull the inner lever.

He was evidently a youngster, for his production was that of a beginner. Raising his head and puffing out his throat, he opened his bill, and, lo! there dropped on the still air a single note.

To me it sounded like "Shine," and, with the sun warming all things, it sounded most appropriate.

The youngster was so pleased with his effort that he tried again — "Shine, shine," he piped. (A thrush always repeats his notes.)

Away over the field from another tree came back an answer. An older bird was there, and he seemed to be applauding my little friend's debut. He seemed to be singing, "Stick to it, stick to it, stick to it."

Up in the tree-top once more came forth the beginner's song, "I'm he-re, I'm he-re, I'm he-re."

And floating again over the fields came the flute-like voice of the more finished songster, "Stick to it; you'll do it, you'll do it."

Of course, the bird may have meant something very different from the words which I set to its music; but such was the conceit in which I indulged.

As I sat there I heard the sound of footsteps, and I saw Raq giving a welcome to Joe, my farmer friend.

Joe is the minder of the flocks, whilst Alan, his brother, looks after the crops.

"Whither away?" I asked gaily.

"Going down to the lambs," he answered, and then said, "Coming?"

"I've got Raq with me," I said, not wishing to excite the ewes by the visit of a strange dog.

"Keep him to heel, and it'll be all right," he said.

I was only too glad to accompany him, for lambs give me a thrill and a delight whenever I see them.

Soon we found ourselves in a sheltered field. On the one side ran a wood, where the keeper feeds his young pheasants. It was quiet and still, save for the wood-pigeons which clapped their wings as they launched themselves into the still air.

The wood is only just awakening to life. At present its tone is a warm chocolate brown. But the honeysuckle is already in tender leaf, and the young nettles are beginning to climb on their upward journey.

The other side of the field rears itself into a big mound, rounded and curved by storms of a thousand years. In the warm glen the ewes and their bleating youngsters were gathered. As soon as we appeared on the scene, it was the signal for a hundred drinks.

Anxious mothers looked up at the click of the gate, saw at once that Joe had a stranger with him, saw, too, with an angry gleam in their eyes, that a strange dog trotted at his heels.

The nearest sheep gave its call, and immediately put itself between its lambs and the dog. She faced it, alert, ready to do battle, and stamped angrily with her front feet on the soft turf. Those sharp, cloven feet and the hard, concrete forehead were weapons not to be made light of.

Everywhere the lambs were scuttling to their dams. Our presence had created a hurricane thirst, and on all sides little woolly bodies knelt down as though to say their grace, their noses butting upwards towards the source of supply.

"Watch their tails," said Joe to me.

They were all hanging as still as catkins on a hazel-bush. Then, suddenly they started to waggle, to quiver with delighted ecstasy.

I looked at Joe inquiringly.

"They've just got the first taste of the warm milk," he said; "it allus has that effect on 'em. Every waggle means a trickle."

Soon the warm nourishment ceased, and a hundred dejected tails hung limply from a hundred lambs that preferred a feast to a sip. "Little and often" is the motto of a wise ewe.

Farther on a little comedy was being played. A lamb ran violently towards a grey-faced ewe that was looking in every direction and bleating out its plaintive call as it turned slowly round.

Up came the youngster ready for the cup that cheers, eager to make up for lost time.

But the old sheep, though looking for her lamb, was in no hurry. As the eager spirit arrived, down went her head towards the woolly mite. For a fraction of a second she nosed it carefully. Then she prodded it away.

The lamb was not to be denied, and sought eagerly to appease its hunger. This time, however, the ewe butted it away with such force that the youngster was almost knocked off its legs.

Again I looked at Joe inquiringly, and he said:

"That's not her own lamb, you see, and she knows it — there are no free drinks in this field."

Then, trotting down the hill, came another wee mite. He bleated out his quavering woe at each step. The ewe swung round, ears turned in the direction of the newcomer, her metallic answer full of solace and encouragement.

Once more her head lowered itself to the bleating lamb, and, having passed the test of eyes, ears, and nose, he was soon imbibing to his heart's content.

I looked around at the hundred lambs that were in the field. Save for a slight difference in marking, they were nearly alike as peas in a pod. I wondered how I should have picked out my own baby if it had been mixed up with ninety-nine others, all dressed alike, and most of them emitting the same music.

So I turned to Joe and said:

"How did that ewe know its own lamb? They all look alike to me."

He touched his nose and said, "You haven't got it here. They smell 'em out. Every ewe has a scent of 'er own. Her eyes may deceive her, she may be taken in by another lamb's bleat, but every ewe knows her own perticler smell, and until that tickles her nose she's on 'er guard."

As we walked on I noticed one little chap was running about as though he had a fur rug tied round him.

"I thought lambs could stand the cold," I said, pointing at the little one's overcoat.

"So they can," said Joe. "I've seen 'em born in a blizzard, and in three minutes they've been suckin' and a wobblin' by the old sheep's side. Once they get on their legs they'll stand a'most anything."

"What's the jacket for, then?" I continued.

Joe laughed and said, "That's an old trick of ours. You see, that lamb's ewe died and left it an orphan. Also, we happened to have a sheep who lost both her own lambs at birth."

"So the bereaved parent was presented with the lonely lamb?" I inquired.

"Aye," said Joe; "but it's not quite as simple as that. You remember what you saw just now — how that old ewe butted away the outsider?"

I nodded, and he continued — "Our job is to get the new lamb accepted as her own, and to do that we've got to give the youngster his new mother's smell."

I turned and looked at the little chap with the wrap on; and as I did so I noticed that his covering was the skin of another lamb. Then the light dawned.

"I've got it," I said to Joe; "you skinned the dead lamb and put it on the orphan, so that he should pass the test of her own smell."

"That's about it," said my companion. "It's not very difficult with a young ewe — you can take 'em in pretty easy. It's the owd 'uns that are the trouble."

And so amidst the bleat of the lambs we sat down, and the new awakening of a sleeping earth entered into our souls.

From the hedge came the "pink-pink" of a bird whose breast was aflush with the dawn, whilst blues and greys wreathed this glowing colour in a glorious nimbus.

"Chaffinch," said I.

"See the two stripes on his wings?" asked Joe, as the bird fluttered to the ground.

"That's his spring uniform," I said. "Every little hen chaffinch in the district will mark his dapper appearance — there are no slovens in Nature."

In the wood we heard the "chik-chik" of an alarmed blackbird. Presently he came and alighted on a fence, and as he did so he lowered his head, and his tail was slowly raised like a drawbridge.

He too was as slick as though he had just been oiled and polished.

"Not much to look at," said Joe, alluding to his dark feathers.

"He's a bird of the shadowed woods and the hedge bottoms," I said. "Look at that bill of gold. It's meant to be a little splash of sunlight that filters through the leaves."

Then from the branches came the song that has a never-ceasing charm. It is only a short one, and can never be mistaken for any other.

The hedge-sparrow sprayed its own little bit of territory with spring delight.

"That's the dunnock," I said.

"I know it," answered he; "little brown bird with a fine bill."

"Smoky grey-blue breast," I continued, "and a suit that never has a feather out of place. Listen to its song. It seldom finishes on a full-stop — always on a comma."

Once again that cheery ripple burst forth inconsequential, with no care in it, and ending with a question, as though it sang, "If winter comes can spring be far behind?"

"Happy are those people who have a garden where the hedge-sparrow sings like that now," I murmured.

"How's that?" asked my companion.

"Because," I said, "where the dunnock sings in March there will be a nest in April, and in that nest will be four little bits of blue, as though someone had sliced the sky and placed the pieces in a cup of moss."

The Bells of Spring

Getting up early has quite a number of advantages. To begin with, it gives the early riser such a virtuous glow. This lasts well on towards late afternoon. Those who arrive downstairs later do so with a half-apologetic kind of look as they meet the breezy individual who knows that he saw the sun rise. "It is the early bird which catches the worm," we say. Until I knew that worms were nocturnal in their habits I always thought it was particularly hard on the worm to be caught first thing in the morning. Now I know that it is the belated worm returning home that is caught. Not the early riser, but rather one which has developed night-club habits — so perhaps he deserves to be penalized.

How I came to be up so early in the morning need not be told. Suffice to say that Raq and I were by the side of the wood when all things were grey, when the wood itself was nothing but a cold dark shadow, and when the hush which precedes the dawn was not broken even by a sigh.

But the beasties of the night know by the universal grey dawn that their reign is over. The fox makes for his lair and the otter returns to his holt. Claw and tooth, often red with their adventures, steal into their retreats, where shadow takes the place of night.

Quite suddenly, the greyness takes on a warmer, pearlier tone, for across the eastern sky there streams a streak of daffodil light. Like a long trumpet it stretches across the heavens, its mouthpiece in the lips of some unseen herald proclaiming that, though sorrow may endure for a night, yet joy cometh with the morning.

Up from the wet meadows the lark begins to soar, and his silvery cascade of song breaks the spell of quietness. Now a blackbird gurgles out from a high elm, a thrush flings out his morning challenge, and then the whole orchestra of the hedges and fields is let loose. A mighty infection runs through every dingle and copse. Warblers, robins, hedge-sparrows, rooks, magpies, finches, all join in the merry roundelay of morn, until the ever-rising sun calls them to the more prosaic work of home-making or of family ties.

Out in the field, and some distance from the wood, I noticed Raq pointing with his nose at something on the ground. As his pendulum was working at a furious rate, I interpreted it that he had found something of interest.

When I arrived on the spot I could see nothing, and I fancied that he must have found the place where a few odd partridges had been lying during the night.

However, as he persisted in his excitement and kept cocking up his eye at me, I looked closer, and then saw that the earth had been disturbed.

Going down on my hands and knees, I soon found a camouflaged hole, and the dog, seeing that I was investigating, immediately began to dig with his front paws, kicking out the loosened soil with the vigorous strokes of his hind legs.

Not wishing to scatter the earth too much, I pulled the dog away, and soon found a burrow running underground. Here at the end was a warm nest of down, and in it I felt a number of young rabbits.

I brought a handful to light. Naked, blind little roly-polys they appeared to me, as unlike the pretty youngsters which gambol at the top of the big burrows as it is possible to imagine. But for them, the doe robs her own breast of her soft fur, and no doubt she thinks they are the handsomest children ever brought into the world.

As I looked at them I remembered the fable of the snipe, who, meeting a sportsman with his gun, implored him not to shoot any of her brood. On his asking how he should know them, she said that he could not make a mistake, for they were the handsomest birds he would meet. An ugly bird got up on the wing, the sportsman's shot rang out — and it was a snipe he shot. For a sportsman's idea of beauty is one thing, and a mother-snipe's is another.

Even so must the rabbit view her youngsters with very partisan eyes. Probably whilst I was delving into her temporary home she was watching me from some thicket. For the doe feeds her young at dawn, and then, covering up and smoothing the entrance of the hole, leaves them till nightfall. On her return they will poke about her with tiny pink noses, and, though they cannot see, yet Nature has endowed them with a keen sense of smell, and it is more than probable that they locate the source from which they receive their milk supplies by the aid of those absurd little noses.

Raq sat by me watching them squirming. His grave eyes had a look in them, however, which told me that I had but to say the word, and those hapless, helpless youngsters would have been transferred into a corridor from which there would have been no return. So I carefully replaced them in their downy retreat, and did my utmost to cover up the tracks and traces of my soil dislodgement.

If, however, the nose of some prowling badger come that way in a night's meanderings, I would not give much for the safety of those helpless rabbits. Neither would he take the trouble to dig out the front door. His sensitive nose would locate from the surface just where the young were lying beneath. A few quick strokes of his powerful spades, and all would be over. "Brocky" would be ambling away with a smile on his face very similar to the one worn by a very oft-quoted tiger.

Later in the day we came across Ned, the postman, and, as usual, received a hearty invitation to accompany him on his rounds. He had a wholesome respect for letters, but a hearty contempt for postcards. He was always annoyed when he had to trail to some distant farm and hand in a printed card.

On the other hand, he would often hold a letter in his hand and say to me:

"If I didn't deliver that 'un, the whole course o' history might be changed."

Then he would tell me something of the two lives that he was linking together, and what might happen if he failed in his trust.

"I'm a livin' shuttle," he would say, "and I'm weavin' these two threads together, and, when the 'piece' is finished, old Ned will have had an 'and in bringin' out the pattern."

Sometimes I found it rather enjoyable when, amongst a particular heavy bag of correspondence, he could not at once find the postcard which he was about to deliver. As he was searching in its depths he would say to the farmer's wife who stood waiting:

"Ah, well; it's just to tell you that Mary and the babby are aw reet, and that she's comin' ovver at Whitsun to stay wi' yer. She says as 'ow she's got all her cleanin' done, and as 'ow — But here it is, at the bottom as usual. But you'll find out the rest that's on it fer yersel' mebbe."

As a matter of fact, had Ned lost the whole batch of his postcards, he could have delivered their messages by heart to their varied owners. But never by any chance did he reveal the contents to any but the destined recipient.

"What a month this is," said Ned to me, as we walked by a certain spinney. "You told me just now as 'ow you saw the first stream o' sunlight shaped like a trumpet. Look at these first spring flowers — ever notice how many of 'em are bell-shaped?"

Even as he spoke there came over the still air, faintly but sweetly, the sound of a far-off peal.

"A weddin' mebbe," said Ned, stopping to listen.

"How the sound swirls and sways," I murmured.

"Look around ye," he cried. "In nearly every hedge ye'll find a nestin' bird. The robin's in the hole in the bank, the wild duck is sitting ovver there on fourteen pale-green eggs, the swallers and the martins are hastin' on their way with the thought of family joys speedin' 'em on."

He paused a moment as though he were weighing up whether he should divulge his inmost romantic ideas. Then he continued:

"Well, it seems as though Natur' fits in with these bridal doings. Look at these early flowers which appear. So many of 'em are droopin' bells, as though Natur' were ringin' 'em on their way. When the west wind blows, I watch the snowdrops, the little woodsorrell of the pine-woods, the tall daffodils, and bluebells, all of 'em ringin' a car — car —"

I expected the old man would fumble about for this word, so I was ready for him.

"Carillon," I said quietly, so as not to interrupt him. But I spoke so softly that he did not quite catch the word, and thought I said, "Carry on."

"Carry on?" he said scornfully, and almost glaring at me for spoiling the poetry of his ideas with such a prosaic phrase.

"Carillon," I repeated in a louder voice.

"Aye, that's better," said he, mollified, and smacking his lips over the word for which he sought. "All of 'em ringing their carillon — bells for the birdies' weddin's, swingin', swayin', pealin'; and the great big marsh marigolds and the flamin' but- 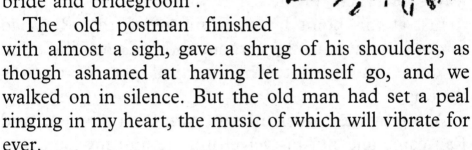 tercups standin' up straight out o' the green grass and holdin' their cups —"

"Chalices," I suggested quietly.

"Holdin' their chalices aloft and cryin', 'Good 'ealth to bride and bridegroom'."

The old postman finished with almost a sigh, gave a shrug of his shoulders, as though ashamed at having let himself go, and we walked on in silence. But the old man had set a peal ringing in my heart, the music of which will vibrate for ever.

As I walked home through the village I happened to pass a well-kept garden, the owner of which I knew slightly. Being full of the ideas which Ned had given me, I stayed for a moment to chat with him as he moved amongst his varied and well-trimmed beds.

I must say I never felt very drawn to the man. Once he had bundled Raq out of his grounds in a rather too forcible manner for my liking. But, with the music of Ned's bells still ringing in my ears, I felt I wanted to pass on some of the melody to someone else. Thus was I ensnared into telling him of the quaint conceits of the old postman.

"Ah, yes," he said in his superior way; "very pretty, no doubt. But we botanists like to stick to facts."

"Facts are not so beautiful as truth, sometimes," I ventured to interpolate.

"Those of us who have a scientific bent explain things differently," he said, with a superior air. "You see," he added, "those tubular flowers of yours live under cold atmospheric conditions. By closing the petals much of the warmth which would be lost by radiation is preserved. The surface presented to the Arctic winds and dews being that of the involucral leaves, or bracts, of the calyx, which —"

Just at this point I saw, to my relief, that Raq had forced his way into the garden, and the scientific mind at once descended to the practical plan of evicting the dog.

Along by the roadside I sat down for a moment, and Raq came and put his velvet muzzle into my hand.

"Raq, old man," I said, "you saved me just now from perpetrating justifiable homicide."

The old fellow knew not what I said, but the affectionate tone caused him to snuggle nearer to me, so that he touched me with every part of his shaggy body.

"Mark the contrast," I continued. "Wedding bells, carillons, golden chalices; and involucral leaves, bracts, calyx — ugh!"

Later, when I reviewed the day and its events with my wife, she finished by saying with a slight shudder:

"That man would typewrite a love-letter."

I felt somehow or other that it was a most apt description.

A Spring Epidemic

"How are your preparations for photographing the rooks going on?" asked my wife at breakfast one morning.

"Oh, quite well," I answered; "they are all busy building and re-building, and many of them are giving the old nests a thorough spring clean, and —"

I never finished my sentence, for a sudden fear intruded itself on my thoughts, and, at the mention of those dreaded words, "spring clean," I looked at my wife, and all my fears were confirmed.

There are certain diseases which show preparatory symptoms, and, as I looked into her eyes, I could see lurking in their depths an unwonted gleam, a smouldering fire which I knew from experience all the waters of Niagara would never quench.

Instantaneously my mind went back to her first question. No, it was not interest in natural history which had prompted her query. The sinister suggestion, "She wants you out of the way," laid its hold upon me.

Like a flash all the expedients by which I had hoped to prevent this domestic revolution passed before me. With what high hopes had I purchased an electric vacuum-sweeper! How diligently had I enamelled white every bit of brass in the house! How gladly had I sacrificed the snugness of coal fires for radiators, and how I had even tried to train Raq to wipe his feet on the mat!

All my preparations and preventives had been in vain. Through every barrage the deadly virus which shows itself by making its victims transport dust from the attic in order to raise it in the cellar, had penetrated. I realized, as I had never realized before, that, though I thought myself the head of the house, in reality I was only the figurehead.

I raised my head and looked at her. "When do you begin?" I said brokenly.

"The lounge on Monday and Tuesday, the front bedroom on Wednesday, the spare —"

"Yes, yes," I said, interrupting her in the details of the campaign, "and the study?"

"Oh," she said with a smile, "when the light is good, and no wind sways the tree-tops, and the rooks —"

There was no need for her to finish the sentence. I knew what would happen. Like a born strategist, she had made her plans.

I turned and went slowly upstairs. "And they are called the weaker sex," I murmured to myself, as I put camera, plates, and changing-bag ready for the day when my hobby would be transformed into an eviction.

When I reached the keeper's cottage I found most of the kitchen furniture outside the door reposing on the small cobbled yard. John Fell was seated on a stool cleaning his gun.

"Not removing, are you?" I asked apprehensively.

He shook his head and said:

"She's just doin' a bit of paperhanging — 'tidying up a bit', as she calls it." Here he lowered his voice and said, "Couldn't head her off from it nohow."

I spoke sympathetically to him, and he shrugged his shoulders philosophically. Then, jerking his thumb in the direction of the kitchen, he quietly touched his forehead, indicating that he put such "carryings on" down to a weakness in that region.

"We were comin' through the village last week," he explained, "and I said to her, 'Did yer see that lurcher dog lyin' outside Smithson's — shall have to keep my eyes open fer 'is doin's.' 'No,' she answered, 'I didn't see the dog, but Sally Stordy and Mary Johnson have their curtains down.' After that she was quiet all the way home, and that's when the fever started — kind o' hydrophobia I call it."

After the gun had been cleaned I went along with him to look at some poultry which he kept in a field some distance from the house. He slipped a couple of cartridges into the breech of his gun, saying that magpies were doing damage to his eggs. As we walked side by side, I asked him whether he had ever noticed birds showing a fondness for decoration.

"Have you ever found them decorating their nests," I asked, "much in the same way as we beautify our houses?"

John shook his head, and replied:

"No, I never have, but a lot of birds deck themselves out, decorate their bodies, so to speak, when spring comes round." He paused a moment and then said, "Ever noticed the cock-sparrow, fer instance?"

"I've noticed that his coat becomes browner and richer, and that his white markings stand out clearer at this time of the year," I answered.

"Aye, that's true," said my companion, "but there's something else aboot 'im that's rather interestin'. Wait till we come across one, and I'll show ye what I mean."

We had not long to wait before John gripped my arm and, pointing to a bird seated on one of the poultry-houses, said, "Look at his throat."

I scrutinized the sparrow, and said:

"He's got a black bib on under his bill."

"That's what I wanted ye to notice," said John. "In November that 'bib', as ye call it, isn't black — it's grey. Feathers overlap one another like tiles on a roof. His November feathers are grey-tipped and the rest of the feather is jet-black. Ye follow me?"

I nodded.

"Well," he said, "as the winter goes on that grey tip wears away, and by spring only the black bib is left. He's very proud of it and shows it off. It's 'is bit o' decoration."

We walked about amongst the hens for a few moments, but no magpie showed itself. Only in the wood somewhere did we hear its mocking laughter.

"By the way," said John, "now I come to think of it, the magpie shows a fondness for pretty things. I've found many a nest, and inside has bin little bits of shinin' pottery — sometimes I found the lid of a tin, and now and then small squares of coloured cloth. That, in a way, is a beginnin' of the decorative sense, isn't it?"

STOLEN FINERY.

"Yes, I rather think so," I replied, "but I can tell you something even more distinctive than that."

"Let's go and sit under yon bush," said the keeper, "and while ye spin yer yarn that old magpie may take it into 'is 'ead to pay the hen-runs a visit, and if he does" — here John glanced at his gleaming weapon — "I'll give him decorative sense."

Soon we were screened from view, and quietly I began to tell my story:

"I was visiting a cemetery which was a regular bird-sanctuary. And as I passed by a weeping willow tree, a storm-cock flew away, throwing insulting epithets at me."

"Nest was there," interjected John.

"Well," I said, "I examined the nest, and was surprised to find that right around it was woven a garland of white artificial flowers which the bird had taken from the wreaths on the graves."

"That certainly is unusual," commented the keeper.

"You see," I went on, "those white flowers really drew attention to the nest, which, as a rule, is the last thing a bird wishes to happen. It prefers to camouflage its home rather than to make it conspicuous."

"True," said he, "that's a case where the bird had a love of finery and decoration. Perhaps from a small beginning like that sprang up that 'how d'ye do' that's goin' on up yonder." He looked expressively in the direction of his house.

"Yes," I said, "it may be the beginning of what we call the aesthetic sense."

We sat on in silence for a while, and I was thinking of the long way that the "decorative sense" had travelled.

I watched the birds that flitted in the bushes and the trees. The little tits performed their gymnastics on branch and bank, clad in saxe-blue and saffron. A cock-pheasant stalked under the beeches, gloriously arrayed in bronzes, golds, chestnut, and I could see the metallic sheen on his throat and cardinal crest on his head. A woodpecker joyously "yaffled" as it spurted from tree to tree — a flash of green and scarlet. All of them decked out in bridal robes — every colour meant to make its appeal to some mate that watched its lord and master strut and fly in woody groves.

Yes! I thought, the decoration of the body came first; in birds, fine feathers; in man, feathers and furs filched from the wild, and then, after a while, trinkets and ornaments.

My musings were interrupted by the keeper, who had been slowly puffing his pipe.

"Ever come across any badgers?" he asked.

"I can't say I'm intimately acquainted with them," I said evasively, so that he might tell me what he had been pondering on.

"Well," said he, "they're a queer mixture. In themselves they're very clean animals — never foul their own burrow. But the queer thing is that sometimes you find 'em livin' in the same hole with a fox fer company. They might as well live in a drain," he added, screwing up his nose at the very thought of living with Reynard.

"And you say that naturally they are models of tidiness and cleanness?" I asked, wishing for more information.

"Aye," he said, "they dig deep underground corridors, and they have their separate sleepin' compartments, and their sanitary arrangements are wunnerful fer an animal."

"They dig down pretty fast, too, don't they?" I queried.

"If you put 'em down on the ground," continued John, "a'most afore yer can say 'Jack Robinson' they've disappeared in the ground. They've got feet like mighty spades, and armed with terrible claws." He  paused to scratch out in the moist earth the kind of track a badger leaves when on the hunt. Then he went on: "They draw down into their sleepin' compartments armfuls of bracken. But arter they've used it some time, they, too, get the turnin' out fit."

"Male or female?" I asked.

"Both on 'em," John said. "Fer on a nice sunny day they bring out all their beddin' into the sunlight, and when it's sweet and clean, back it goes again. That's the beginnin' o' the cleanin' mania, I reckon. Yer can find in animals nearly every trait that's in human bein's."

"Naturally," I said, "all big rivers start from tiny springs."

When I arrived home I found my wife, for the time being, quite normal again, and over the tea-cups she said:

"And what did you and John Fell find to talk over this time?"

"Oh, about the decorative spirit which is found even in animals and birds," I answered, careful not to mention the cleaning business, lest the smouldering fire might blaze forth afresh.

"How interesting," she said. "And what conclusions did you come to?"

"We decided," I said slowly, "that in almost every case the male was naturally the finer and more beautiful creature."

"Indeed," she said quietly and with an emphasis that ought to have warned me to go warily, "and did you find that this was true when applied to human beings?"

"Well," I said, as lightly as I could, "we felt that the mania for dress and ornament, scarves and furs, was indirectly a great tribute to us menfolk — it might be looked at as an attempt to borrow what Nature has not provided — the idea of the equality of the sexes," I added, rather pleased with the way the argument had turned.

"You being 'Beauty unadorned', I suppose," she said. "I see."

We were quiet for a moment or two; then, as I rose from the table, she said sweetly:

"I'm quite convinced you are right. That reminds me. I think I'll go and *spend* a week in London with my people."

As I went out at the door she blew me a kiss from her finger-tips, saying:

"An attempt to borrow what Nature has not provided. I must remember that when I'm at Selfridge's."

I walked slowly upstairs, whilst the ominous word "spend" rang in my ears, and from my study heard her humming gaily the Jewel Song from *Faust*. Alas! my arguments had been too convincing!

The Fringe of the Road

There had been a shower or two during the night, and Raq and I found the woods rather damp. But is there anything fresher on earth than the smell of the woods and fields after a gentle spring rain?

Everywhere the bluebells were adorning the copses with purple scarves. Their emerald stalks sparkled with moisture, whilst the rusty bracken of last year's growth acted as a wonderful foil to the delicate beauty of the bells.

All things were rejoicing in the morning sun. The wood-pigeons left the pines with tremendous clatter, and for sheer joy stalled upwards towards the sky. Once a squirrel, startled by Raq, scampered in haste towards a mighty, sleek beech.

I looked upwards for a few moments expecting to see him watching me from some fork thirty feet up. But, instead of that, I discovered him only four or five feet from the ground, with the trunk of the tree towards which he had run screening him from view. On being discovered, he hurried upward with quick, restless jerks, whilst his tail seemed to be used like a pump-handle, undoubtedly helping him in his climb.

On the edge of the wood the hawthorn was dusted white with opening May-blossom, and already the languorous scent was being wafted through shimmering glades.

About a mile from the village I came across Jerry crouching by the side of the road.

As soon as he saw me he placed his finger on his lips and motioned me to take my place beside him, also to call Raq to heel.

"What corrupt practice are you up to now?" I whispered to him smilingly, after he had gripped my hand in informal welcome.

We were nestling right in the midst of gorse-bushes, which already were beginning to give a foretaste of the golden harvest they will display a few weeks hence.

In answer to my question, Jerry motioned to me to peer through the bottom of the hedge, and, some fifty yards away, I saw a fine hare lopping casually towards the road, on the fringe of which we were hidden.

"What dark designs have you on her?" I whispered.

The old rascal put on an injured look, and then, handing me his glasses, told me to scan the hedge-bottom that rimmed a wood about a quarter of a mile away.

I took the glasses, scrutinized the distant spinney, and then shook my head, for I could see nothing.

"At the foot of the withered larch," he whispered cautiously.

I found the mark indicated, and, after much searching, for it is not the easiest of matters to steady binoculars for any length of time, I saw a small patch of ruddy brown.

"Fox," communicated my friend, "watchin' 'her hareship' make for the road."

"But the hare won't lie in the road?" I said incredulously.

Jerry nodded his head emphatically.

"Yes, she will, and fox knows it too," he said quietly but decisively.

"But I thought that a hare lies in a 'form' on some fallow or grass land."

For answer Jerry looked through the hedge, and then very cautiously peered through the bush up the road. Then he motioned me to look also, and there, in the middle of the track, sat Puss. She was facing us, and about forty or fifty yards away. Very busy she was with her toilet. First of all she carefully dusted the soil from her strong hind legs.

"A hare 'ates fer soil to stick to the fur on its legs — that's what allus happens after rain — allus makes fer a

quick-dryin' road where she can 'ave a wash and a brush up. You watch her."

I did as I was told. The hare very leisurely groomed herself. After the back legs were to her liking, she sat on her haunches, and, with her front paws washed her long ears with their black tips. Finally she combed out her long whiskers — those long, sensitive antennae which telephone immediately to her brain whether a hole in the hedge is big enough for her to rush through.

"Take the glasses and look at the withered larch again," urged my companion *sotto voce*.

Once more I peered through the hedge-bottom at the distant copse. The red patch had vanished.

"We shall see some fun if we wait here a bit," whispered the old poacher. "Like jugged hare?"

"Where's the fox?" I answered, ignoring his question.

"Don't know exactly," said he; "but I'll be bound he's gettin' to the windward of her. He'll know where she is a'most to a foot within a few  minutes. That nose of 'is'll get her scent from sev'ral points, and he'll soon reckon it out where's she's sittin'. He's scrattin' along on his belly somewhere at this minute. Only 'opes as how he strikes a place atween us and the hare."

We sat still for a short time. Puss still cleansed herself, but now more spasmodically. She would appear to settle down to enjoy the morning sunlight, and then would suddenly give some part of her body a final polish.

"Can't she see you?" I asked my friend, as he watched her through a small opening.

He shook his head, and said:

"Fortunately she's facing us square. A hare can't see very well right in front of it. Eyes are set at the side o' the head, so that she can see back'ard better than for'ard. As a rule, nothin' gets in front of her — she's

101

too speedy. Her foes are nearly allus behind 'er. That's why 'er eyes are set like that."

"Why don't you give her warning and frighten her?" I whispered, feeling sorry for the timid creature that was being stalked by sudden death.

"'Twouldn't be fair," answered Jerry decisively. "If 'e can git 'er, 'e ought to 'ave 'er. If she's caught nappin', so much the worse fer 'er. It's the way o' the wild."

Very cautiously (and I admired the dexterity with which he moved in that confined space without the crackle of a leaf giving the alarm; he slithered more like a snake than a clumsy human being) he again glanced through the hedge-bottom — this time, not towards the distant spinney, but up the side of the hedge which would screen the skulking fox from his victim.

"I believe he's atween that clump of 'olly and gorse," he said, jerking his thumb in the direction in which he had been looking. "If so, we shall see the fur fly in a minute or two. Keep yer eyes glued to that hole so that ye can see it. A flash o' red fur, gleamin' like blood in the sunlight — the arrow of death — the snappin' together of jaws like a steel-trap, a cry like a wounded

soul in the torments of 'ell, and afore the dust 'as cleared away — no hare — no fox."

I kept my eyes riveted on the unsuspecting, timid creature that lolled in the balmy air. My heart hammered so loudly that I felt sure it would send its thumping alarm to her with whom lay all my sympathies — a wild bundle of timid elegance that would never do any harm in her life — a sleek —

But I was not able to finish my thoughts, for suddenly a small bird in the hedge on which my gaze rested creeked out a solitary note. The sound was small but metallic, and grated with subdued passion. But it was enough for the hare.

Almost before the note had ended she wheeled round, raised her ears, and, with a terrific bound, went racing at topmost speed up the road. She did not stay to investigate whether that alarm were true or false. Even as she moved the hedge became alive with small birds. That one creaking alarm was the signal for every bird within sound of its note to scream out its vindictive dislike against what had caused it.

"Jenny Wren spoilt 'is game," said Jerry aloud to me. "Look, he's away back again to the spinney."

Across the field, in full view, and with a bunch of small birds following him, all hurling at him epithets of the worst description, slunk a very disgusted fox. His tail hung limply behind him. So near had he been to success. Another moment of quietness, and Puss would not now be prancing over sunlit fields. Would she have learnt her lesson? I wondered.

"That's about the nearest squeak I've ever seen," said Jerry to me, as we walked towards his cottage. "That little Jenny Wren is a terror to every hunter, and especially a fox. Another minute and we'd a found (he put special emphasis on the found) a dead hare, and then there'd a bin soup and red-currant jelly on the table at the manse, I reckon."

"Found?" I said, looking squarely at his laughing, deep-set eyes. "You mean poached," I added.

"Found," he corrected, "and on no man's land — found on the King's highway. 'Death by misadventure' 'ud be the verdict."

"I'm glad the hare escaped, anyhow," I said.

"Which is no denying o' my statement," said Jerry, with a smile, and then, very gravely, he added in a tone altogether different from any I had ever heard, "My forefathers owned all the land as far as your eyes can reach."

For a moment he looked round on the fair terrain that shimmered in the sun; then I thought, as he looked curiously at me, he sighed, and said, "I'll tell ye the story some day mebbe."

Just before we left him to push on to the village, he said, "Don't fergit now, whenever there's bin a shower o' rain, and the day turns out sunny and warm, the place to find interestin' things is on the road that dries the quickest. Ye'll find the partridges and the pheasants dustin' themselves. The rabbits, too, will be a doin' what the hare was, and 'where the body is' — What's that verse in the Bible?"

" 'Wheresoever the body is, thither will the eagles be gathered together', " I quoted for him.

"Aye, that's the verse. And where the wild things loiter, there ye'll see them that's after 'em. The wild's a queer mixture of life and death. And," he added slowly, "if it weren't for death lurking round the corner, there'd be precious poor specimens of life. Ye can work the thought out fer yersel'.

"So long," he finished, waving his hand, and I heard his cheery whistle grow faint, and finally lose itself in the distance.

Nature's Tools

As Raq and I passed by the farm, I noticed a small group bending down and looking at something in which Sally was interested. The three men proved to be the keeper, Joe, and Alan.

On joining them, I found they were admiring a hen and her chickens.

"Come in this mornin', she did," said Alan to me, pointing to the brood.

"She walked up to the kitchen door," said Sally, "as proud as could be of these little 'uns. Never knew she was 'sittin' ' — must have had her nest yonder by the wood. But they're a fine lot, and no mistake."

"They always are," said the keeper, "when they 'sit' themselves. Nature knows how to look after them better'n we do. Think o' the trouble we have with a sittin' hen. There's the findin' of a suitable place; then there's the feedin' and the time she has to be off the eggs. Even then the results are not o' the best."

"We civilize too much," commented Joe, "and that means coddlin' and ends i' weakness."

"You know Jim Goodley up at Feud Nook?" asked Alan.

"Knows everythin' there is to know aboot hens," said Sally — "or thinks he does," she added as an afterthought.

106

"Well," said Alan, "I went up t'other neet and he was sittin' at a table with a score o' eggs in front on 'im. He took fust one and then another, and dangled what looked like a ring ower 'em.

"'What are ye doin', Jim?' I said.

"'I'm findin' oot which'll 'atch oot cocks and which'll come oot pullets,' he said. 'You keep yer eye on t' ring, and if it swings in a circle over the egg, then a pullet is in it, and if it swings like the pendulum of an owd clock, then, sure as life, there's a cockerel inside.'"

"He was usin'," chimed in the keeper for our benefit, "what they call a sex indicator — but get on with yer yarn."

"Well," said Alan, "he put aside fourteen eggs, and he said, 'These go under the old broody in the mornin''.'"

"What's happened?" asked Sally, having, no doubt, visions of a poultry run full of nothing but egg-layers. "Are they out yet?"

"Oh, aye, they're oot reet enough," said Alan, with a grin. "They hatched oot last night, and" — here he paused to allow the interest of the group to grow — "every one on 'em are cocks."

All of us had a good laugh at this *dénouement*, and Sally said, "Must a' gotten mixed up wi' the ring's movements, I reckon — good job they weren't calves or lambs he was fiddlin' with."

"Best to leave Natur' alone," added John Fell. "If we could all 'ave what we wanted it 'ud be a queer world to live in."

Sally went indoors to her house-work, and for a few moments the rest of us sat and watched the chicks.

Presently the hen settled down, and the "cheepers" sought the warmth of her feathers. As one of them peeped out, Joe said:

"Look at that little white speck on the end of his beak." And, as others showed themselves, he added, "Why, they've all got it. I never noticed it afore."

"That's the fust tool that Natur' presents 'em with," said John Fell.

We all turned expectantly towards him after he had made this remark, and, seeing that he had roused our curiosity, the keeper continued:

"Have yer ever thought how many o' the tools which we humans use have bin copied from the birds and animals?"

Alan characteristically raised his cap and rubbed the back of his head as he said, "Can't say as I have, anyhow."

"That little white speck," continued the keeper, "if yer feel it, yer'll find it as sharp as a bit o' flint. And when the chick is ready to come oot into the world, it scrapes this against the top end of its imprisoning shell. It acts a'most like a glass-cutter's diamond, and in time it cuts the hole through which the little 'un escapes."

After a bit of manoeuvring with the hen, Joe caught one of the chicks, and, on examining it closely, we found it even as John had explained.

"Ye can see it on most o' young birds," the keeper added, "plovers and curlews and gulls, and, when I see it, I never cease to wonder at the way Natur' fits things out fer the life they 'ave to face."

We left Joe and Alan to get on with their varied work. But the dog and I went on with the keeper who was anxious to visit a certain covert.

Overhead the rooks were continually flying backwards and forwards from the fields to where their mates were sitting high up in the elms. They were hard at work finding food, and we could see the big pouches underneath the bills bulging out with grubs and wireworms.

"Ever examined a rook's bill?" said John to me, taking for granted that I was thinking of them.

"I know that there is a bald patch at the end of a rook's beak, and that this is its distinguishing mark from crows and ravens," I said.

"Aye," said John, "that's right enough, but at the moment I'm thinkin' of it as a tool. It's made for diggin' in the hard earth. It's built to get at the roots o' things. Shouldn't be surprised if man didn't get his idea of a pick from them knowin' birds."

Our attention was drawn to Raq, who was prancing round a thick bush. We judged that a rabbit was lying in its "seat" within its dark shadows.

I was about to call the dog to heel when John said, "Let 'im have a run, it won't hurt him or the rabbit."

So, in a moment more, away dashed Bunny at a fearful rate, ears lying low on the back and body pressed as closely to the ground as possible.

As for the dog, he followed behind like an old tank, and finally pushed his nose as far up the hole down

109

which the rabbit had bolted as it would go. With this he had to be content.

"Play much football when ye were at school?" asked John.

I nodded, wondering what on earth he was going to ask next.

"What did yer put on the bottom of yer boots?" he asked.

"Why, studs, of course," I answered. "You couldn't keep your feet on a wet day if you had flat soles."

John turned to Raq and whistled him, and, as he came obediently to heel he said, "Take a good look at his paws and tell me what you notice."

I did as John suggested. At a word the dog rolled over on his back, and, taking hold of his feet, I began:

"Pads, hair separating them, strong claws unsheathed —"

"That'll do," said the keeper, as I mentioned the claws. "What do yer think them things are for?"

"Well," I said, feeling them, "they are evidently no good either for fighting with or for holding the prey as a cat grips a mouse."

"Ye're on the right track," the keeper murmured.

Then his question concerning my football-boots occurred to me.

"Why," I said, "a dog chases his prey. Speed is a *sine qua non*."

"Never heard of it or seed that thing in my life," said John.

"I mean," I continued, "that a cat stalks its victims quietly, then springs on them unawares. Speed, except

110

for the final spring, is not a necessity. But a dog without fleetness of foot would starve."

"Ye're quite right," said the keeper, "and so, because it must run ovver all kinds o' ground, wet and dry, hard and soft, Natur' puts football-studs on its feet to keep it from slippin', and to help it in turnin' fast. It's another o' them kind o' tools I was tellin' ye of — or, at least," he added, "it's another of them fitnesses which Natur' never fergits in the equippin' of 'er children.

"As a matter o' fact," said my companion as we paused before he entered the covert, "if people would only keep their eyes open, they could tell from the looks of a bird many o' the ways in which it lived."

"You mean," I said, "that Nature has adapted all animals for their particular mode of life."

"I mean," said he, "that their bodies grow accordin' to the way they are allus usin' 'em."

"That function creates organism," I added.

"Aye, that's the proper way o' puttin' it, I reckon," said John, with a smile. "Here's a sparrow feeds on seeds and anythin' it can pick up. Natur' gives to it a pair o' thick nutcrackers — a general purpose tool. Put a plover's bill on to a sparrow's head and it would be dead in a week. For the plover or tuwhit needs very fine forceps fer pickin' up small insects from the grass."

"Talking of tools," I added, "reminds me of the lobsters I used to catch under the rocks. I suppose we got our idea of pliers from them?"

John nodded. "And our chisels and planes are fashioned like the teeth o' rabbits, our needles copy the thorns or the spines o' hedgehogs. Cushions were fust

111

on the feet o' the hunters as quietening pads — cats, foxes, otters, and such-like. Carry on," added the keeper.

For a moment or two I conjured up in my mind visions of birds and beasts with which I am acquainted.

"Spoons," I said, "were first thought of by the ducks — they shovel up mud and water and then sieve it through the saw-like edges of their bills."

The keeper said, "Right. And spades?"

"I should think that we got the idea of such a tool from the badger," I conjectured.

"Probably," said John. "He can dig hisself in inside o' three minutes." Then he added, "I won't ask yer to come into the wood with me this mornin' — Raq might disturb any nestin' couples, you know. But I've given yer something to think aboot, I reckon."

As we tramped homewards I found myself examining with new eyes everything that moved. I was asking myself what we had learned from the wild things which flitted and moved before me.

I saw the heron rise from the river, and remembered the spear-like bill with its rapier point. Then I heard the tap-tap-tap of the woodpecker as it hammered out its hole prior to commencing nesting operations.

The sight of a thrush intrigued me most. She had a large snail in her beak. True, she could not use her bill as we do a hammer. But she found a large stone, and on it she broke the shell, and carried off the contents to some hungry youngsters.

As I passed the blacksmith's shop and heard the clear note of the anvil, I could not help saying to Raq, "Raq, old chap, that heavy lump of iron in there is only a thrush's stone improved upon."

He looked up at me, wagged his tail as much as to say, "I don't understand all of what you say, but, if you say it, it is so." What a companion!

I go a-Fishing

I have met many anglers, but none to compare with my friend John Rubb, either for quaint knowledge concerning the ways of fish, or in the patiently persistent way that he fishes for them.

He has come to that time of life, moreover, when he can say with a smile, "If fishing interferes with your business, well — give up your business." This makes him a leisurely man, and no-one will ever make an angler who is in a hurry.

To look at, John is not imposing. He, although always tidy, gives the impression of being tousled. His broad forehead is crowned with hair that has seen better days. Usually he wears a trilby hat in which a few artificial flies disport themselves. His blue-grey eyes have a "yonderly" look, and gaze at you as though you were out of focus. Only when you mention the river do they begin to dance and gleam.

His memory is of the best and worst. For Trustees', Leaders', Quarterly Meetings he has a "forgettery" rather than a memory. But never in my life has he ever failed to keep an appointment with me when the rendezvous has been some sequestered pool or turbulent stream. I have agreed to meet him miles from home, at all hours of the day and night, in deep ghylls, on rocky heights — but never once has he failed at the appointed hour to step out of black night and give me the call for which I listened — sometimes the alarm note of the wild duck, or the challenge of a cock pheasant.

He is, too, a naturally silent man. When the time is ripe, he can open out and bring from his treasure-house things new and old, but he can also tramp by your side for half a day and, save for an occasional staccato observation, never open his mouth. This is friendship indeed.

It was a beautiful spring morning. A warm, westerly breeze was blowing just enough to move the daffodil bells in my neighbour's garden. The sky was grey, with patches of blue showing at intervals. In my study lay a mass of papers which spelt business. Above them lay a trout-rod. Outside, a starling mocked at me for being indoors, and, clipping his wings, sang of the delights of the open fields.

I put the papers on one side and determined to seek out John Rubb. I found him in his shop, in which were three or four customers.

Now I never go straight to the point and ask him whether he will come fishing with me. We both act on the tacit assumption that we are far too busy to go, and finally merge into making definite plans.

"Nice morning," I murmured, as he served his customer.

"Not too bright," he answered, glancing outside.

"Westerly breeze," I said casually.

"Well," said he, looking at those in the shop who were still to be served, "come back in half an hour and I'll attend to you."

And so joyfully I returned home, donned my old brown suit, packed up the necessary equipment, and within the hour we were whirling away in John's Ford.

As we left the town I caught sight of my wife, and waved to her a gay farewell. A little farther on John caught sight of his wife. She also was making her way to town.

"By the way," he said, letting the pedal slip into high gear, "what reason did you give her" — here he jerked his thumb in the direction of my better-half — "for going off to-day?"

"Oh," I said, "I told her that you needed a day off and badly wanted *me* to go with you. What did you say on the 'phone to yours?"

John grinned and said: "I told her that I thought things were getting on top of you, and that you badly *wanted me to go with you*. Those two are bound to meet and —"

"There'll be some explaining to do when we get back," I said.

"It's worth it," was his comment, as he inhaled big lungfuls of spicy air.

We tackled up — that is, we put our rods together and donned our waders — about a hundred yards from the river. For a few moments we sat down and enjoyed the silence, which the varied sounds enhanced. High in the trees the wood-pigeons cooed out eternal love to their mates. Above us a tiny speck flew in swift spirals and circles, and, as it swooped downwards, made a curious sound that reminded me of the bleat of a goat with the tremulant stop of an organ behind it.

"Snipe," said John. "The wood-pigeon sings his love; the snipe plays to his mate on a musical instrument."

"Doesn't he make that noise with his throat, then?" I asked.

My companion shook his head. "He makes it as he dives earthwards," he explained. "His outside tail-feathers are stiff, and the wind turns them into a kind of a harp."

We sat and listened to it for a moment or two, and then John said:

"The cricket, you know, is an instrumentalist also. He scrapes his leg against the rough side of his wing. He was one of the world's first violinists."

As we moved quietly towards the stream, my companion said, and I knew he was giving me advice in an indirect way:

"Fish can't hear sounds very much. You can sing or shout all day and it won't disturb 'em. But they're very sensitive to tremors of the ground. If you put a worm on top of a plant-pot full of soil and stand the pot on the piano, even you could sing and the worm wouldn't appear annoyed."

He gave me a quick glance to see whether I were sensitive to remarks made about my voice.

"But," he continued, "if you strike a note on the piano, that worm will soon burrow out of sight — the vibration of the wire has reached it and given it warning."

He was silent for a moment or two, and I knew he was giving me time to make my own inferences.

"I've known fellows come down to the river and stamp about with their heavy brogues, and then wonder why they've caught no fish. They forget that they'd advertised their presence, and that they were dealing with wary folk. Expensive tackle, and the latest thing in ball-bearing reels, don't make up for the loss of ordinary precautions."

As we came nearer the river I heard a sound, and turned towards my companion.

"Hear that water-hen?" I said.

John shook his head.

"No water-hen that," he said. "That's the call of a frog that's fairly bulging out with spring ecstasy."

I walked down quietly to the water's edge, and found that he was correct. As I returned, my friend asked:

"Ever think of the time when there was no such thing in the world as a voice — only the sound of the wind in the trees, the crash of the thunder, the melody of running water, the roar of the cataract — all voices of inanimate Nature?

"That frog over there," he continued, "was the first animal to stretch a string over its throat for the breath to play on. The frog's call was the first voice in the world. That was the beginning of our Galli Curcis, Melbas, and Adelina Pattis."

"Think of it," he went on. "Hundreds of thousands of years ago — a voiceless world. Then this little amphibian, awakening out of his winter sleep, where he breathed for months through his skin, suddenly opens his eyes on a spring world. He wants to find a mate, and Nature, in the course of the years, supplies him with the necessary instrument."

"It wouldn't be much of a voice at first, would it?" I asked.

"Certainly not," John answered; "just a quaint little croak which caused his mate to try and gurgle out a response. And to-day nightingales, blackcaps, thrushes, oratorios, operas, and jazz find their beginnings in a frog's throat."

"Behold how great a fire a little matter kindleth," I quoted.

"That's true," said my companion, "especially when it is linked up with emotion."

We arrived at one part of the river where the stream came down with considerable vigour.

"No good," said John; "trout are not strong enough to face that torrent this time o' the year, and in the quiet part over there the sun throws your shadow right across the water."

We moved around the bend. The water was shallow our side, but across the stream the bank was high and the water deeper. Here and there bushes screened it from fierce light.

I sat down for a moment or two to watch my friend.

Very carefully he walked into the water, giving his rod a few preliminary flicks.

"Rod must be part of your arm, an extension of it; not another separate member," was a favourite dictum of his. Also: "Make the rod do its work; that's why it's springy; and keep your elbows slick with your body. You are not throwing stones at the fish; you're casting a gossamer line."

I noticed that at first he did not wade in very far, and he spent a moment trying the nearer shallows. I should have waded in and prospected the deep water at once.

A moment later I saw him netting a nice half-pound fish.

"Never neglect, but don't waste time on the unlikely places," he said, as he dropped the fish in his creel, "and" — here he paused and looked at me — "be ready for the unexpected, for, in fishing, it's that which always happens."

After that we parted for a time, and fished our various ways. But if angling itself has a thrill, so have its accessories.

To begin with, when standing knee or waist deep in water there is the gurgle of the stream making melody against your waders, and every gust of wind comes to you laden with spring spiciness.

Then, too, standing truncated in the water takes much of the fear of the wild things away. They see you in an unusual position, and do not recognize you as "man, the monster and enemy."

The dipper curtsies on its stone in the flashing current, his white breast gleaming like a crescent star. By the margins of the pools the grey wagtail walks with dainty steps and flicks his tail jauntily. Sometimes the otter steals from his holt, and, frightening your fish, swims like a brown wraith upstream.

Later on, John and I met for a belated lunch.

"Had any luck?" I asked.

"A few," he answered laconically.

Now, when John in answer to my question says, "Never had a pull," I know his creel is really empty. If he says, "An odd un or two," I know that means quite seven or eight. But if he answers "A few," then I am certain that a couple of dozen shining beauties have been caught.

Just as we opened our various repasts I thought I heard him say something.

"What was that you said?" I asked.

"It was the fisherman's grace," he answered.

"I didn't catch it," I persisted.

So, doffing his battered trilby, and whilst the lark carolled overhead, he said:

> Lord, suffer me to catch a fish
> So large that even I,
> In talking of it afterwards,
> Shall have no need to lie.

Signposts

We certainly had tramped a long way, and I felt a trifle wearied. Raq was as fresh as paint. I wonder how far a dog really travels when his companion has done about seven miles. I think it would be fair to multiply the distance by three or even four.

We were toiling up a lengthy hill of rather steep gradient. The dog was revelling in the varied scents left behind by the furry creatures of the field and hedgerow.

I was busy wondering what sort of a race the world would look on in about two thousand years. Here is the problem on which my mind turned:

Granted that function begets and modifies organism — viz., the curlew's bill has grown long and curved because it has had to poke about for centuries in the ooze and mud, whilst the wood-pecker has grown a tongue of telescopic length so that it can probe in the deep recesses of bark — what will human beings develop into, who, more and more, allow trams, cars, and taxis to do the work of their legs? To put it in the other way: If neglect of functioning causes organism to atrophy, will the race become in the course of the centuries human "dachshunds" with short legs?

I had not answered the question when, before me, at the junction of two roads, stood a signpost. I walked up to it to read its instructions.

One hand pointed to "Lone Pine", the other to "Woodsome".

Many words have a magic in them. Some are woven of the finest lace; others gurgle as running water. Some are distilled from the dew; others have been carved out of solid rock. But who could read of such places as "Lone Pine" and "Woodsome" without smelling the cathedraled aisles of stately trees, or seeing the vision of pale anemone cups catching the mossy flavours of moist banks?

So intrigued was I by the names on the signpost that I knew not which way to turn. I stood like the ass of Buridanus, which was placed between two bundles of hay of the same weight, same flavour, same appetizing odour — and which died of starvation; but he was an ass!

Underneath the post, the grass grew green, so I compromised by sitting down beneath it, and, becoming drowsy by watching the long ribbon of road up which I had toiled, I think I must have reached not the fortieth, but the thirty-ninth wink. Then I heard a voice speaking, and I noticed that the voice was answering the question that was humming in my own  mind — "Lone Pine" or "Woodsome"? It was low and sweet like the lullaby of the four winds, and I was certain the voice proceeded from the signpost:

"I can only direct; I cannot compel," it whispered.

Still the question hummed in my own mind — "Lone Pine" or "Woodsome"?

Once more the quiet tones of the signpost caught my inner ear:

"I am only of use to those who know where they want to go."

Aye, that was the trouble, I thought; I could not make up my mind as to my destination.

Then again the signpost stirred, and I heard it say:

"The joy is in the travelling; not in the arriving."

That is true, I said, rousing myself; "getting there" is very often better than "having got there".

Then I turned and looked at the wooden philosopher for a moment. I could have sworn that on one of the arms was printed: "This is the way; walk ye in it."

I rubbed my eyes in wonderment. But, when I looked again, all I saw were the outstretched signs, "Lone Pine," pointing to the heights; and "Woodsome," stretching out towards the valley.

Leaving our resting-place, Raq and I struck across country and dropped down towards the village which we often visit.

We heard the cock-grouse chuckling at his own jokes, and saw him raising his head above the heather on which he feeds, watching our every movement.

I stood for a few moments listening to the sounds which oft-times go unappreciated. Sounds which, when one is close to them in the valley, are merely noise, float upwards and reach the heights with a music peculiarly their own. The air smooths their edges. The slight breeze imparts to them a finer tone.

The children's laughter tinkled like a brook. A rooster crowed out his challenge in a farmyard, and the distance lent an enchantment of peace to the call. The quackings of ducks, the distant baying of the dog, the low rumble of a train screened by the trees, the cheerful whistle of a ploughman with his team of steaming horses — all very ordinary sounds — wafted in gusts from low-lying fields, made a harmony with the whisper of the rustling grass on the heights. The old signpost had stated the truth — "The joy is in the travelling; not in the arriving."

I was brought back to earth again by seeing Raq scamper off into an adjoining field.

I found him there giving what I call his "second-best affection" (the first-best he reserves for me, and never by any chance bestows it on anyone else) to the familiar figure of Ned, the postman.

I joined him, and as we walked along I told him about my soliloquy with the old signpost.

"I wonder who thought of setting up signposts in the first instance?" I said. "We know precious little of many public benefactors."

Ned shook his head in answer to my query, but replied:

"The principle is as old as Adam."

I looked at him to see what he meant, and he continued:

"Nature's had her signposts fer thousands o' years."

I looked around me to see whether he was alluding to anything which could be fitted in with his statement, but, finding nothing, asked him to explain.

"Well," said he, "I'm a-thinkin' of the bees. They're born travellers, you know; but travellers with an object in view."

"They are on the look-out for the honey-filled —"

"Nectar-filled," corrected my companion. "The bees don't find honey ready-made. They distil it into honey themselves — but ye've the right idea, anyhow.

"Now, where was I?" he continued, his tone indicating that I had shunted him from the permanent way on to a siding.

"Signposts," I reminded him.

"Oh, aye," he continued; "well, these little foragers set out to find the nectar. Now, take notice how they set about it."

The old man stood still, his eyes aglow with the thrill of his theme.

"For the first week or two the young bees are the nursemaids in the hive. Then the great day comes when they are fitted to go out into the wide world which they've never seen. What's the first thing they do?"

I shook my head, and waited for him to continue.

"They leave the hive and circle up aloft above it. They're like homing pigeons making note of every landmark that shall help them to spot their home. I see them makin' this flight, and I know their little brains are saying, 'There's a white gate — that's to the left of the entrance board. There's the red chimney of the farm — the hive's half a field away'; and so on."

"The world becomes a wheel to them," I ventured to remark, "of which the hub is their hive and every landmark a spoke which leads from the distant circumference to it. Chimney and gate are the signposts."

Ned looked at me admiringly. "Book-larnin' is a wunnerful thing. Wish I could put it like that. Howsomever, as yer say, with the 'hub' in their minds, off they go on the search."

He paused for a moment, and I could see his eyes were far away, following in thought his beloved bees. By way of reminding him that I was still on the earth I gave an apologetic cough.

"How do you think they find their source of supplies?" he asked. "They see some flashin' petals twinklin' red, blue, or yeller, and every colour is a signpost of Nature's and signals to 'em the message, 'Fill up in me'. "

"There is no poster, 'No Soviet Petrol Sold Here', is there?" I asked.

Ned smiled. I knew he would forgive my flippancy, for it showed him that I had caught his simile, and he was rather proud of what might be called his topical allusions.

"Then," he continued, "as soon as they fly down to the glaring sign, how do you think they know where the hidden store is? Remember, they are youngsters fresh to the work and havin' no experience. They read the handwriting on the walls, which gives them full directions."

I looked puzzled at his last remark, and, rather gratified, he explained.

"Ever noticed what you call the markin's of flowers?"

"Yes," I answered, "I have noticed stripes and dots and —"

"Those lines and shadows are the handwriting on the wall. They are Nature's signposts, saying to the bee, 'This way to the nectar-well'. They are the flower's paths, honey-lanes if you like, and at the end of the lane lies the fairy distillery."

As we walked on we passed a wood. It was full of the mystery of late afternoon. Already the wood-pigeons were returning to their roosts, and, though the amber light still twinkled through the topmost boughs, yet around their bases shadowed peace reposed.

Nailed to one of the trees on the fringe of the wood was a notice, "Trespassers will be prosecuted".

"A bit o' bluff," remarked my companion, pointing scornfully at the signboard. "Trespassers can't be prosecuted — you can only be prosecuted if you've done damage which can be proved. Ever seen that signpost hung out in Nature?" he asked.

"Which one?" I queried.

"That warnin' one there," he answered, and, without giving me time to reply, he added, "You fight shy o' nettles, don't ye?"

"Of course," I replied; "they sting pretty severely."

"And you know 'em when you see 'em?" he asked.

I nodded.

"So do the animals. They get stung, perhaps when they're young, and they don't require a second warnin'.

But there's another plant which grows near 'em called the white deadnettle. It's quite harmless. It could be eaten by anything alive without damage. It has imitated the leaves of the stinging-nettle, and to protect itself makes its leaves speak to all foragers, saying, 'Trespassers will be prosecuted' — but it's a bit o' bluff, for the leaves can't sting at all. It's a warnin' signpost that means nothin' — a cartridge without any shot in it, like that writing in the wood."

Just before we parted he said:

"But there's one sign you never misread, and that's a wasp's. You never mistake 'im fer a harmless insect, do ye?"

"Never," I said, glancing at several parts of my anatomy which had tender reminiscences.

"Those yeller stripes are Nature's trespassin' notices," said Ned. "They say to all and sundry, 'You touch me at your peril'. He flies about in a football jersey so as to impress himself on your memory. He's conspicuous so that he may be avoided."

As I walked home in the gloaming, with the thoughts raised by the signpost in my mind, I rested for a few moments by the hedgeside.

Here and there snowdrops glowed like faint stars. What a thrill these first wild flowers bring to those who find them!

White as untrodden snow are their fairy bells, reminding us that frost and ice have been their matrix.

But the heart of each flower is tipped with green, the first-fruits of the year. It points forward — "To

129

lengthening days, singing birds, smiling fields, and hedges robed in emerald" — such is its signpost of promise.

A Neglected Sense

I had made some comment to my wife, and, though she did not say it in so many words, yet I gathered that she did not agree with my remarks. She sniffed.

Of course, she would repudiate at once that she had been guilty of such a vulgar nasal indiscretion. But, all the same, I am quite sure something did happen, and the proof of it lies in the fact that our conversation languished.

Raq had caught that soupçon of a snuffle, and looked at me with pained, expressive eyes. He probably felt that his own monopoly had been invaded — the nose belonged to his domain.

I felt that I could not overlook the incident, and determined to administer a rebuke, and that I would do it by education rather than by dictation.

"Raq, old man," I said, "there was a time when human noses played a most important part in our daily existence."

My wife said nothing, but it was at this point that she found it necessary to carry things out of the room. But she left the door open — which encouraged me to proceed with my plan and to speak a trifle louder and with more deliberation.

"My ancestors," I continued, "scented out their enemies and located their dinners by means of the efficiency of their noses."

At this point my wife reappeared, wearing a bored expression, and looked carefully round the room to see what else she could carry out — to replace later.

"The nose," I went on, keeping my eyes fixed steadily on Raq, "played a more important part than the eyes — that is why it occupies such a prominent place. It is a receiving-station, advantageously placed on a promontory which juts out from the mainland. Hence it receives the messages of the breeze long before the lenses of the eyes are brought into action."

The dog shuffled nearer and pushed his muzzle affectionately on to the palm of my hand.

"Your nose is moist, old boy," I said. "That means it is more sensitive to impressions than when dry. Its moistness sometimes causes you to sniff hard and long."

Here I was conscious that my wife had found something else which needed to be taken to the kitchen. But I also noticed that she did not hurry through the open door, so I continued:

"Moist noses are extremely useful — in animals."

Judging by the quiet that prevailed in the kitchen, I felt I could proceed with advantage and profit, so I went on:

"Nowadays, old fellow, the nose has fallen from its high estate. Its colour" — here I raised my voice a little

— "is of more importance than its function. It is now not even an adornment — it is an anxiety. To present it 'unshiny' and 'unspotted' to the world is the ideal of its possessor."

I believe at this point I distinctly heard something being put down in the kitchen, if not with violence, certainly with decision. So I said:

"I think we had better go for a walk, old chap."

We made our usual preparations, and, just as we were starting out, my wife came to me and said:

"Don't forget to take a large handkerchief with you, my dear." She paused, and, looking at Raq, shook her finger admonishingly and added, "Moist noses are extremely useful — in animals."

She walked sedately back into the dining-room, and I could not help but wonder if my ancestors also had the art of tilting theirs.

I suppose it was only natural that my thoughts should revolve around the theme of the morning. Such phrases as "Putting one's nose out of joint" and "Being led by the nose" kept coming up before me.

Then I began to think of the world outside my own senses. How much pleasure I should lose were my nose to lose its power of response! I began mentally to write down a list of those scents, fragrances, smells which give me infinite pleasure.

There is the scent of a distant beanfield in flower. You are tramping along the lanes, tired and dusty, and with a parched throat. Then the breeze stirs gently the tops of the hedges and brings with it hardly a scent,

133

certainly not strong enough to be called a fragrance — shall I call it a bouquet of Nature's sweetest wine — angels' breath — distilled rainbow? No words are delicate enough to describe it.

And what of the clean mustiness of the earth upon which a short sharp shower descends at the end of a burning day? "Like a field which the Lord hath blessed," says the aged Isaac, as he catches the scent of the clinging nuttiness which pervades the raiment of Jacob's borrowed robes.

And what shall I more say of the incense of a pine wood, of the smell of the cows as they pass on their way to the byre, of the gorse spraying the hills, of the gusts of honeysuckle at dusk, and last, but not least, of the fragrance, subtle but real, of the curly hair of your own dappled child?

What a sense of reality would be imparted to our Church prayers if instead of thanking God for "mercies received" and "blessings enjoyed," we were to say, "We thank Thee for the green fields and clover blossom, for marigolds glowing like the sun, and for violets hidden in the hedgerows!"

I would like to have introduced the word "nose" into that prayer, but unfortunately it is not poetical enough. And yet "Rose", which is very much akin to it in sound, is the theme of every poet. Strange!

I came across Jerry later in the day. He was sitting on an old log, making up flies for the trout season, which will soon be opening.

"March browns?" I asked, looking at his tackle.

"Aye; water-hen and purple, with a partridge and orange for the tail fly," he said, handling his handiwork affectionately.

Then there assailed me a curious heavy smell. It reminded me of coughs and colds and paregoric.

Jerry noticed that I had caught the scent, and said: "Aniseed — been catching rats last night. They love it," he added.

"How does it work?" I said.

"'Tices 'em out, and then I nip 'em wi' my fingers at the back of the neck. I sit there in the dark, and they come out fer it," he said, as though he was describing the most ordinary of proceedings.

"Some animals are perticularly fond of certain scents," he continued. "Ever kept any red valerian in yer garden?"

"Yes," I said, "I think I have."

"Ever noticed, when you've bin goin' yer rounds in a mornin', that it's been crushed down?" he asked.

I nodded.

"That's cats as 'as done it. They revel in it. If there's little about, they'll come fer miles to roll in it. Why, I don't know, 'cept as they must like it."

"Red valerian" — the word unlocked something in my mind. Away down in the depths of memory something stirred and gradually came to the surface, and I said:

"Do you remember that story of a woman who broke a flask of perfume over the Master's feet?"

"Aye," said Jerry, "it's a favourite o' mine. I liked that bit where it says, 'And the house was filled with the fragrance'."

"Well," I continued, "the red valerian comes from the same family as the precious spikenard from which that perfume was extracted. It cost about twelve pounds to make that gift."

Jerry looked at me for a moment, and then, bending down to the tying of his flies, he said quietly:

"There's a big difference between 'cost' and 'worth'." Then, holding up a fly, he cried, "Cost — a penny. Worth?" — here he made a few imaginary casts with a rod, each time landing an imaginary trout and putting it in his creel. "That's what it's worth," he cried, with his eyes aglow.

As I went home in the eventide a man met me, carrying a large net. At first I thought he was an angler, and by way of introduction I asked where he was going to fish.

He almost shook his net in my face as he said:

"I'm not a fisherman; I'm hunting for moths."

Now I know nothing about such creatures, save that they work havoc in blankets and furs, so I asked him whether he found such a hobby exciting.

"They are the most wonderful creatures in the world," he said, with enthusiasm. "Why," he continued, "had I been a moth I could have smelt your coming towards me when you were a mile away."

I think I must have looked rather incredulous, but, with the zeal of an enthusiast ever ready to make a convert, he laid down his tackle and proceeded to enlighten me.

"Ever seen an emperor moth?" he asked.

"Never," I replied; "at least not that I know of."

"It's a king dressed in browns, old gold, and beige," he said ecstatically. "Can you spare a moment or two?"

"Willingly," I replied.

"A few nights ago," he continued, "I caught a female of the species, and, wanting to examine her, I put her into a box and left her on the mantelpiece of my den, whilst I wrote a letter or two. The night was starry, and a gentle breeze stirred the alders by the pond. Happening to glance up at the window, I saw a beautiful sight. Fluttering against the pane were half a dozen emperors, their eyes glowing like live coals and their markings almost incandescent against the outer darkness. You are interested, I see."

"Go on," I said.

"Why had those brown beauties appeared so suddenly?" he asked. "How did those fluttering wraiths come to be seeking admission to my den?"

I shook my head and confessed ignorance.

"The little empress in the box," he continued, "had broadcast her scent. It had floated out into the night air. It had been borne on the breeze until the delicate antennae of the emperors had received that fragrant S.O.S. They were there in response to her silent but potent summons. They had scented her out, though separated by darkness and space. That is what I meant by saying that, had I been a moth, I could have smelt your approach when you were a mile away."

"Marvellous!" I said, with genuine amazement. "And the antennae, those delicate feelers, are the noses of the moths, are they?"

"That's about it," he said, picking up his net, and vanishing into the deepening shadows.

I walked home, wondering still more at the world in which I lived.

I looked at Raq, and saw him interpreting a world of smells and scents which were beyond my senses, even as the ultra-violet rays cannot be caught by the lenses of my eyes.

Just as I was envying him, a car flashed by me, leaving a reek of petrol behind it.

A SCENE IN COURT!

Then, on entering the town, there hung about a certain street the oily sickliness of a fried-fish emporium.

This latter experience brought me to earth with a jolt. Would I really like to have a sense as subtle as a moth's, living as I do in a world that has discovered petrol and fried haddock?

On the one hand are the flowers, and on the other hand are the drains. Sensitiveness to one means being sensitive to both. I am glad that I have not to make a choice. Perhaps even having a dry nose has its advantages.

News

As I walked through the village which lies as peaceful as a pool at the foot of the fells, I found myself humming "Oh, it's quiet down here."

I love its leisureliness. There is a sense of timelessness that pervades all things. True, the clock of the old church booms out the hours, but in such drowsy fashion that you never feel the days are speeding by: rather that they are unfolding, and that there are plenty more to come. The inhabitants are few in number, living their own separate lives, and yet, in another sense, they are a very select company, and this circle has its own conscience, its own outlook, its own ritual.

There are three ways in which you may become an integral part of that community. You may settle in the village and enter into its life. At the end of twenty or twenty-five years you have served your apprenticeship, and the fact that you were once an outsider is forgiven, but never forgotten. Or you may have the good sense to marry one of its inner circle. You are then known as the husband of Sarah Graham — "Jim Bell's lass that was, ye ken." This is your passport to its inner life. But to enjoy the real "freedom of the village," you must have been born there. All others are in reality only co-opted members.

The only thing that travels fast in this little community is "news." Something happens in an isolated farm — a new baby gives its first cry; an old sow has farrowed; "Ben Scott has heerd from his nevvy in Canada." Before the sun has dispelled the morning mist every home is enriched with the news.

How is it done? Keen eyes have seen the marks of the doctor's car on the road that leads to the distant farm. A certain foreign stamp shouted out the secrets of the letter, and someone saw it in the bundle of missives that Ned was carrying as he went his rounds. As for the old sow — wasn't there a light showing in a certain sty at eleven o'clock last night, and what could that mean but that the little grunters had arrived?

That morning, as Raq and I paid our respects to certain of our friends, we learnt that a big parcel had arrived by post at Mary Johnson's, and that Sally Stordy had actually received a telegram. I left the village behind and pushed on to open country, but I knew the little comedy that would be played in the village before nightfall. Members of various households would suddenly find that they needed something at the shop. There, the arrival of the parcel and the telegram would casually be commented upon. If no news of the contents was forthcoming, one of the neighbours, as she passed the recipient at her door, would say in an ingratiating tone, "Hopes as 'ow there was somethin' good in yer parcel, Mary?" or another sympathetic member of the C.I.D. would murmur to Sally, "Ye've not 'ad bad news I 'opes this mornin'?"

Good folks all of them — sometimes, perchance, a trifle envious — always curious, but ever ready to build their little cantilever of friendship to meet yours from the opposite bank. Their very curiosity at least makes you feel that you stand for something in the corporate life; there is nothing more lonesome than being one of hundreds of thousands — one, in a big city.

Walking along one of the by-paths of the woods we came across the keeper. We found that he was about to pay a visit to the under-keeper who lived on the far side of the estate. So we joined forces.

We walked on in silence. When I am with Ned, the postman, we spend the time in talking. But when I am with John Fell, I wait for him to talk.

"You can't both chatter and see what ye should," he has said to me many times. "It pays me to keep my eyes open."

He stooped down to look at the carcase of a rabbit, or, rather, all that was left of it.

"Stoat?" I asked.

He shook his head, and answered, "Carrion crow."

Then, picking up the remains, he pointed to the skin of the legs. It was rolled back so that it reminded me of the way in which a lady peels off her long gloves.

He held up the head, and I saw that the eyes were missing.

"I must be on the look-out for that gentleman," he said. "He's particularly fond of eggs, and it'll not be long afore he'll be able to get busy."

Down by the river he glanced at every creek.

"That's my mornin' newspaper," he said, pointing at the level stretch of silver sand.

I looked at him with a question in my glance, and he pulled a paper out of his pocket.

"This," he said, holding out the printed sheet, "they tell me, is run off by the thousand every night in some works i' London. How do they get their news?"

"In a hundred ways," I said; "but much of it by telegram, telephone, cable, and even by wireless — then it is set up in type."

"I get mine," John continued, "from little bays like yon, from the soft clay banks and muddy paths, and, best of all, from the light falls of snow in winter time."

He motioned me to follow him down to where the sand glittered in the morning sunshine, and pointed at various mouldings left there.

"Heron," he said, tracing with his finger a big three-toed impression. "He stood there last night or early this mornin' as still as a stone — stood there fer a longish time, never movin'. With his slate-blue feathers he looked like a mixture o' grey dawn and smoky dusk — couldn't tell 'im from a shadder of the night or a reflection o' the day."

He looked up as he spoke, and I asked:

"How do you know he stood there a long time?"

"Look how deep the tracks are," he answered. "He's stood still and long, and as he's stood so he's sunk deeper in the sand. I'll show yer his shallower walkin' tracks somewhere else."

"Sound reasoning," I commented.

He walked a yard or two upstream, and then called out: "See here," at the same time pointing to little marks by the margin of the river.

I stooped, and saw what looked as though gnomes or goblins had spread out their hands, leaving a delicate impress behind.

"Rats," he explained; "big brown 'uns on the hunt for any refuse washed up by the stream. See where their long tails have slithered o'er the mud?"

Again he pointed to the pad-marks, and said: "Do you see how they all stop dead here? You can see they've turned round and scampered back fer their lives."

He paused to point at those three-pronged impressions a few yards away.

"They were comin' down quite jauntily," he continued, "comin' nearer to sudden death, only they didn't know it — sudden death standin' like a sphinx, and with a bill that can move as swift as an arrow and as strong as the kick of a horse."

"What pulled them up short?" I asked, looking at the little bunch of pad-marks.

"They got wind of him in time: their whiskers fairly curled wi' fright, and fer a second they froze into stone. Then they turned, and the darkness swallered 'em."

"Anything more of interest?" I asked.

He looked round for a moment, and then said:

"The old yarn (heron) didn't go away empty after all."

He stooped, and gave me a little shining disc which lay on the sand.

"That's the scale from a chub," he said, as I examined a golden circular jewel. "A big 'un too, I fancy."

John chuckled, and added:

"I'll bet that old gentleman with the long bill went away and sat on a tree with a very meditative expression in his eyes, with a big 'un like that inside of him."

"Well," I said, "that's a fine way of getting news. Given a yielding, smooth surface, then the foot of every  bird and beast is transformed into type. In glaring headlines and small print they register their doings until every creek becomes a 'stop-press' edition." After a moment or two I added, "John Fell, head-keeper to Sir Lawrence Darte, of Kirkonby Hall, editor of *Nature by Night*."

John shrugged his shoulders and made a movement with his hands as though he deprecated such praise — but he was pleased all the same.

As we were returning in the late afternoon we saw an immense flock of starlings. There were thousands of them. They flashed by with a rustle and a rush.

"Watch 'em," said John; "ye're a'most watchin' a miracle."

I kept my eyes on them. They were a solid, compact mass, tail almost touching the beak of the following bird, and with hardly an inch of space between individuals.

"If ye had a pound fer every bird that's up there, ye wouldn't need to worry over yer pension," said he.

A marvellous sight I witnessed. With speed undiminished they swerved and dived, now they wheeled to the right, now to the left. At one time, when catching the rays of the westering sun, they merged themselves into such flashing reflections that they seemed to vanish altogether. The whole army seemed to be governed by one mind. When they swerved, they swerved with the precision of a single unit. When they dived, not a bird swayed out of its course by a hand's-breadth. Solidly, gracefully, swiftly, precisely, they carried out their aerial evolutions — ten thousand birds with but a single thought.

I was brought to earth by my companion asking, "Who gives the orders?"

I looked at him, not quite catching the meaning of his question.

"Thousands of birds," he continued. "Not a rabble, but a perfect disciplined army. Who gives the orders to turn or dive? Who's the commander-in-chief? How do they get the news to swerve or wheel?"

I had not thought of that. But I said:

"There must be an acknowledged leader amongst them."

"They couldn't hear the pipe of one starling giving orders," he said. "He'd need to blow a bugle to be heard."

"They may arrange what to do beforehand," I said rather lamely.

John shook his head.

"Well," I continued, "you asked the question first. How do they do it?"

"Don't know; nobody knows. We can only guess," said he.

Then, as the birds rushed on, he added:

"It may be due to what they call telepathy: perhaps there's a leader that wirelesses his commands."

We watched them volplaning, nosediving, side-slipping, and then sweep down to the reeds in a lagoon.

"And not a bird out o' place," I heard my companion mutter.

But how they spread the news as to their intended twists and swerves has still to be discovered.

As I entered the town that evening, all the sights I saw gathered themselves round the dominant theme of the day.

Paper-boys were selling the latest edition to eager buyers. Groups of listeners gathered round the shops' loud-speakers, as they circulated the doings of the larger world.

In the streets were small gatherings of neighbours gossiping about the life of their acquaintances and friends. All were eager for news.

Then I had a vision of half-empty churches, bored listeners, listless congregations, and I wondered whether the messages delivered there had the quality of news — the "Good News."

I heard, too, another Voice saying, "It is like a sower — like leaven — like a merchant seeking goodly pearls." Everything He saw was a film, rich with beauty and life. No wonder they said, "No man spake as this man". Always news.

I began to wonder whether my own repertoire of messages were in reality only a museum — a fifth century MS., not a stop-press edition.

Everlasting flowers are, I suppose, better than no flowers at all. They can stand in a vase with a ghastly stare — past fading and past blooming. But it is the spring daffodils which attract the bees.

Companions of the Stillness

When one begins to speak of the beauty of Nature, there are numbers of people who at once begin to rhapsodize over what they have seen in the Lake District, in Italy, or in Switzerland. How few there are who see or appreciate the loveliness of the near-at-hand!

Our towns and cities are not exactly beauty-spots. In the clear light of noon they often appear sordid and garish. Shops, offices, warehouses, streets, churches, long rows of houses as regular as a piano keyboard, give to the mind the sense of distaste and even confusion.

Yet as soon as the sun sinks behind the horizon, then Night, that supreme artist, begins her transforming work.

I like to watch her throwing a soft veil of evening over offending colours, summoning her handmaid Dusk to curtain unseemly proportions, whilst Twilight and Shadow hasten to do her bidding by covering harassing details, until nothing remains but simplicity of outline and the splendour of misty masses.

Night is a wizard touching even our dingy streets and unsightly buildings with soft mystery and shrouded charm.

But to feel her utmost seductiveness one must leave the highways of man for the great open world, where meadow and copse, vale and hill, present her with a fair canvas for her effects.

Have the hours of the day been hectic? Has the speed of modern existence left you jaded, dispirited? Here is a door of escape from the mental hounds that still pursue — here is Nature's rest cure, without money and without price. Ye who go to distant climes in search of the Blue Bird; ye who seek relief from strenuous hours by plunging into still more turbulent recreations — you are coming with me to where my caravan stands under the shadow of the pines, and where my tent looks like a big white moth, as it gazes at the river which is toying with the lingering light of a western sky. Here will I introduce you to my "companions of the stillness".

It has been a cloudless day, and darkness is coming, bringing with it a sense of relief. What a doom it would be to live in perpetual sunshine! As the evening hours steal on I see the rooks returning to their roosting-place, their lazy "caws" giving place to excited cries of admiration and wonder as for a few moments they swerve and dive, side-slip and volplane high in the air above their final resting-place. They seem as though they wish to use up any energy which the toils of the day may not have called upon.

Then, as the robin trills out his evening litany from a neighbouring bush, I turn my attention to the camp-fire. All day it has smouldered, kept alight by four big logs radiating from a common centre like the

149

spokes of a wheel, and finding a continuous glow-point at the hub.

Now I rouse its slumbering heat and pile on wood — not beech, elm, or ash, but resinous pine — pine that has for years imprisoned all the fragrant, wayward flavours of the forest and now is ready to release them for my special benefit — or, rather, our special benefit.

Raq, of course, is with us, seemingly very lethargic as he lies within that evening glow. Only his nose betrays the fact that he is keeping in touch with a very interesting but unseen company which moves stealthily in the bushes beyond the light.

"Light your pipe, my friend. No! not with a match. Stretch forth and take that glowing branch, and, as you do so, catch the scent of its nutty incense, and look at those cathedraled aisles which lose themselves in the wood's inky shadows."

Though I know every foot of ground around the camp — yet the fire transforms the scene. Every flicker and flare resets that rustic stage where the pine-trees stand upright and independent, where the alders shiver deliciously in every breeze, and the great oaks stretch down at me their long, octopus-like arms. Everything is beautiful, but fantastically beautiful. You are in the land of gnome and elfin frolics: the flicker of the fire gives them the rhythm for their feet.

"Put your pipe down for a moment or two, my friend, and give your sense of smell a balm after the petrol reek of the city. You are in a world of dews and fragrances. The honeysuckle in a near hedge is distributing its largesse. Hoard it, accumulate it for the

150

day when you are weary of tarmac roads. That gust which sweeps down the lane yonder is the bridal gift of the meadowsweet — it is as delicate as a tint. Underlying all is the mossy moistness of the good brown earth, like 'a field which the Lord hath blessed'. Rest your head on that log, and, as you sip the flavours, you will feel that a rainbow has transmuted its colours into the perfumes of night."

On the night air there comes the hoot of the owl as with silent flight he searches the grasses. It is full of melancholy and soft menace.

"He is after field-mice, voles, rats," I whisper. "Think of them taking cover as they hear that 'hoo' in which sudden death lurks. Flight, as silent as a moth — wings, merely muffled oars — wide-open eyes like balls of fire, searching, searching, searching. Every mouse shivering with apprehension under the nearest leaf, and praying that the bogey-man of the woods may pass by."

Up in the field by the side of the wood there floats on the night air a long-drawn-out squeal. It cuts the darkness like a knife. There is fear in it, helplessness too. It quavers into piteous, ominous silence. I feel like crossing myself and praying for the soul of the departed. *Requiescat*: poor Bunny!

"Stoat and rabbit," I murmur. "Stoat has done his work quickly and well. Cruelty? Perhaps some other time I can satisfy you on that point — or help to. Listen!"

"Yap — yap — yap." It came from the sombre wood itself, short, staccato, imperious, and yet lonely.

"That's a fox," I interpret, "and he's giving notice to any vixen that he is tired of bachelordom, and is willing  to love, honour, and obey. The vixen sees to it that Reynard carries out his promise! If he doesn't find her here, you will hear the call in a moment or two about half a mile away. Sorry you can't hear her reply. It is no love-sick sweet answer, but weird and blood-curdling, as though ghouls were torturing the soul of some poor prisoner. Ready to move on?"

We leave the fire and its glow, the three of us — you, the seeker after simple joys, Raq, and myself.

"Crook-crook," comes a sound from underneath the bushes. It is raucous, and yet has in it the sound of maternal anxiety. As we make our way it is repeated, this time further from us.

"That's a moor-hen — water-hen, most people call her — calling her chicks to a safer refuge. Little black balls of down, with scarlet tips to their beaks," I whisper.

After a time we find a snug shelter and settle down, all except Raq, who is restless because every bush is alive with life, and a thousand trails are coming to his nose, telling him of the delights of the hunt.

Suddenly a whistle floats down the cool river, and I lay my hand on your arm to ensure stillness. The dog hears it too, and I know the fur is rising on his neck.

"Otter," I murmur quietly, "on the hunt in the pool at the bend of the river. Wish you could see him. There is a rock which rises above the water, and there he will take his kill. If he's finicky, will only take a bite out of the shoulder. If hungry, will eat the whole caboodle, beginning probably at the head. If it's an eel, may begin at the tail. Wish you could see him enter the water again from the rock. Uses his tail like a back-pedalling brake, holding on to the surface of the rock with it.

"Getting bored?" I ask.

"Bit chilly," you reply. I look at my watch, and find that it is almost the time for the dawn to appear.

"Wait a bit," I say; "most wonderful part of the night yet to come."

Even as I speak, and only for a few moments, the whole world swoons into stillness. All Nature holds her breath, and the only sound is the beating of your own heart. The darkness appears to grow more intense, and chilly isolation numbs your spirit.

Then a cold shiver runs through the trees, stirring their topmost leaves, which rustle like the whisper of a ghost, and the silent pool at your feet breaks into little whorls of disturbed water. It is the tide of night at the full.

It is the hour when sleepers turn uneasily in their beds, when the cows in the meadow cease their calm, regular chewing of the cud and move restlessly, as though unable to locate a lurking foe; when little fledgelings in the nest feel for the touch of the mother bird's covering feathers. It is the hour when feeble life

153

in the sick-room ebbs out, or catches the turn of the tide and flows back to health.

"Did you feel that something," I ask, "just an influence tiptoeing through slumbering night? It is Nature beginning to turn back her counterpane of darkness, banishing the hunters to their lairs, and warning all sleepers that the daffodil dawn is about to appear."

Now a cock in a distant farm flings out his morning challenge, and the plaintive bleat of a sheep splits the silence of a distant hill.

Darkness is giving place to misty greyness, and the trees are beginning to emerge from massive groups of sombreness into graceful individuality.

Hark! from a neighbouring elm there is the first songster of the dawn. "Dew, dew, dew! Be-quick, be-quick, be-quick!" sings the thrush. It is the opening aria, and by the time that these few opening bars have been sung the whole symphony of Nature rings out in disorderly sweetness — night has departed.

We are back at the camp by this time, and I have tucked my visitor into a comfortable bed in the van.

 As for myself, I turn into the tent and fling myself on to a mattress. The dog prepares to curl himself up at my feet, watching me as I creep between the blankets.

"Raq, old man," I say, "you have had an uninteresting night. I had to keep you to heel, and you are feeling rather aggrieved. I can see you are wondering what you have done to be treated thus.

For answer he merely shuffled a little closer to me, whilst his tail gave a feeble jerk from side to side.

"You are a dog, old pal. You have little past and no future — no great storehouse of memories. Life is an intense present with you. But your master lives in a city, and spends his life in talking out his soul to other souls who hardly know they are hungry.

"When he grows wearied with interminable meetings and ponderous campaigns, and his own soul has grown thin, he leaves the voluble hubbub far behind and seeks out his companions of the stillness.

"You can't understand me, old chap, but here's a bone for you. It has a nice lot of meat on it. Hungry? So am I, that is why I am here."

I turned over and went to sleep, only to see that verse, "And there shall be no night there". I believe I was disagreeing with the author of it. But, of course, it was only a dream.

SUMMER

Caravanning

Whenever I mention to any one the fact that I spend my holidays in a caravan and tents, ninety-nine per cent of my hearers answer in the same way: "Ah," they say rather wistfully, "that is what I have always longed for."

I have no doubt that at the back of their minds there is a certain idyllic picture of such a life. They see the August sun streaming down in splendour on grassy knolls and making deep shadows under the trees. They think of meals eaten in the open air, where the breezes waft about those spices which are usually sung about at foreign mission-ary anniversaries. Very few ever think that for such a holiday to be a success a certain temperament is demanded, and one or two of the party must have certain qualities. To begin with, unless you wish to "pig it", there must be one member of the camp with a naturally tidy mind.

The caravan is twelve feet by six. It is divided into kitchen and dining-room. It has a stove, drying-cupboard, wardrobe, store-cupboard, shelves, sink, and a hundred other things that are usually found in a house with many rooms. It is, in fact, a tabloid home. Therefore, to ensure comfort there must be a place for everything, and then everything must go back at once into that place. A very similar state of affairs exists in the tents where we sleep and the tiny "bathroom" that is shaded by a miniature tent.

Of course, when I am off alone with Raq, with a small tent packed on my back, with the moors stretching out before me and no human dwelling for miles — then things are different. Economy in weight and comfort is demanded, and how I live then only the dog knows, and he never tells. But in a holiday camp things have to be managed differently.

In our family my wife is the tidy person. She has an orderly mind.

"Can you tell me where my collar stud is?" I ask.

For a second she turns the eyes of her mind on her inner card-index, and answers: "You will find it in the chest of drawers in the caravan on the left-hand side in the smaller leather case." Then she may add something which was not entered on the card-index: "You left it in the empty butter-dish on the dresser, you know, dear."

From which you will gather that my quality of tidiness is not of the same high level as hers. Also you can infer from such an incident how useful it is to have a dog who can tell no tales.

Of course, for a home to have two with such a disposition for orderliness might not be for the best. Were I similarly gifted with such a mania for tidying up I should, were I to pass through the kitchen and find one or two cooking utensils lying on the table, immediately put them back on to their lowly shelves. This might be trying for the cook.

Then I could foresee both of us secreting a duster in some pocket in order to flick off the slightest speck of dust which we met with as we moved about the house. Also we should get to the stage where, before entering, we should both of us change our boots or shoes and creep in on slippers. The time might come when, in order to keep everything spotless, we might sleep out at a hotel to save soiling the sheets. From which you will gather that I look upon myself as a corrective to over-scrupulousness.

Looked at in another way, I am a contributor to her happiness, for if there were nothing to tidy up, her light would be hid under a bushel. How comforting!

When day has swooned into the arms of still night, then the tent awaits us. We light the storm lamp, and, as we walk towards its open flap, the beautiful silken creatures of the night air flit around its brightness.

Within two minutes I am in bed, revelling in the shadows which the lamp casts upon the sides of the tent. As a foil against this flickering warmth is the vision that can be seen through the open flap. The light catches the leaves of a neighbouring tree, and they twinkle like small mirrors. Behind them stretch out dark branches, swarthy arms of some giant octopus always reaching out, reaching out, ever grasping, but never holding.

Behind them lies indigo night, and on her dark bosom heaves the filmy necklet of the Milky Way, a coronet of blazing stars, far away, lest their brightness blind the eyes of mortal men.

But if there is poetry and romance there are other things too. My wife takes longer than I do to snuggle between the blankets. There are tiny black specks on the sides of the tents, some of them just over her bed. These must be examined. They might be beetles.

"Now see you put them away tidily," I say, ducking my head under the clothes. "Pick them up and put them on the grass outside. 'A place for everything and everything in its place'."

"What's that?" she asks, pointing to some moving object on the wooden floor.

"That," I answer, "is a ferocious beast more terrible than the tiger, more to be feared than the panther or the shark — it is an earwig."

She shudders and hops into bed with alacrity.

"Did you look in your bed?" I ask, just as I turn out the light, and seeing she has settled down quietly.

"What for?" she asks sharply.

"Oh, nothing," I answer casually. "Only I noticed —"

"Noticed what?"

"That you hadn't examined it, that's all. Good night, dear, and don't forget that weasels and stoats, foxes and rats, and all the little creatures of the night are more frightened of you than you are of them."

For a few moments longer we lie quietly listening to the noises of the night. Meanwhile I take up the rôle of interpreter.

"Kevit, kevit." The sound comes from the adjoining field, not raucous, but mellowed by distance.

"Owl," I murmur, "probably the short-eared one, flitting like a ghost over the field, and every mouse and vole shivering with fear as the big-eyed one floats past.

"That's the fern-owl or goatsucker," I say, as a low, churring note intrudes itself. "He's after the moths. Opens his mouth wide like a great net, and seeks rest by lying flat upon some bare branch."

Away in the distance a shot rings out. Its echoes roll down the glen.

"Poacher?" asks my wife.

"It may be," I say, "but more probably some keeper is keeping watch over his young pheasants. Many of them are not yet roosting in the trees where they are out of harm's way. He is there to ward off prowling vermin."

"It's not the known, it's the unknown that is rather uncanny," she says, as she finally turns over and settles down to peaceful sleep.

For a few moments longer I listen to the voices of the night. Down through the velvet dusk there falls the double pipe of a passing bird. A moment later an answering call comes, a plaintive single note.

"Curlews," I mutter to myself, "making for the coast where the tide will leave long reaches of wet sand."

In my mind's eye I can see the birds with their long, curved bills reaching out towards their feeding grounds, the leader every now and then giving the note that tells the rest "All is well." Perchance the answering call is to assure the company that in spite of the darkness and the speed there are no stragglers.

After the curlews come the oyster-catchers or sea-pies. In the darkness nothing but dark blurs which for a moment blot out a star and are gone. But in the daylight they are in startling black and ivory uniform, whilst an orange bill splashes them with continual sunlight.

My mind dwells on the sea-pies. I remembered how disappointing my experience with them had been. I had found a nest with four speckled eggs lying amongst the sandhills. It had been difficult to distinguish which were eggs and which was gravel. But I had erected the hiding tent hoping for the best, only to find that the birds were too shy, and to save desertion I had moved on.

With the next nest I had similar ill-luck. Finally, however, I found a nest belonging to a pair of bold birds. Very soon they accustomed themselves to the curious growth which had sprung up in a night and kept moving nearer to their treasures.

Then, on the morning when, after carrying all my heavy impedimenta, I had reached the tent, hope singing in my heart, I had glanced at the nest, my expectations had all been dashed to the ground — the eggs were broken. A sheep had walked right on them. Only a pair of disconsolate sea-pies hovered on the sandhills, emitting at times a note which had in it all the elements of reproach.

With such reminiscences in my mind, I went to sleep, only to dream of unbreakable eggs, oyster-catchers which met you on the sandhills and conducted you to their invisible nests, and scorning such a necessity as a hiding-tent, posed for the camera in as many interesting positions as they could think of. Alas! it was but a dream!

In the morning over breakfast the family chat cheerily over the prospects of the day. At least they do this after they have exhausted the tale of their night's adventures. It usually consists of how they evicted daddy-longlegs, heard various wild beasts seeking to find admittance to forbidden territory, of various moths and midges which tried to snuggle down on their faces.

Then the question arises of how the day shall be spent. Secretly I hate this part of the proceedings, for I do not like to know how I shall spend the day. To have it scheduled out and the hours allotted for various enjoyments is misery to me. I prefer to set out like Abraham, not knowing whither he went, and yet finally coming precious near to the Promised Land.

Finally, all vote to go to the seaside. Of course, I am outvoted and submit, though I gaze anxiously at the hills to see if I can find a cloud, even though it be no larger than a man's hand. But the horizon holds no promise of rain and I am forced to predict a day of sunshine.

For the next three-quarters of an hour the camp buzzes with relentless activity. Certain necessities must be taken. Everyone, too, drawing on past experience, remembers something else which would make for comfort on the beach. It goes down on the list, and usually finds its way into father's pack.

Inside, the van is like a caterer's kitchen. The kettle is steaming; thermos flasks loom in the offing; piles of sandwiches await their wrappers.

Then comes the offensive for the bathing requirements. Each child, having contracted the habit of sitting down in the sea just when its rubber protection has been taken off, must have two changes of raiment — towels, buckets, spades, "woollies" for warmth, paddling shoes, bathing costumes, rubber caps, rugs, books for reading.

Finally, everything is ready, and under a relentless sun the caravanserai sets off looking like a brood of ducklings, father bringing up the rear in order to pick up stragglers and stray packages. I look back at the camp. How peaceful it all seems. Beyond is the brook where the dipper will be curtsying on its stone near the waterfall. Over the hill a kestrel is quartering the dry ground and swooping with unerring flight at its vanishing quarry. I can see the tops of the pines gently swaying in the morning breeze, and know the quiet of its glades, broken only by the small chatter of the tits and the drone of a million small wings.

But the beach lies ahead, where the promenade is littered with people who spend their time in moving from one seat to another, where all the excitements of city life are exaggerated, where cinemas and pierrots, dances, and theatres, tennis and golf, make the sea with its glory just an after-thought, an accessory to pretty frocks, an excuse for herding together round its golden strand.

As for me, I usually deposit my family near the tide and forget the conventional mob round about me. We sport in the sea, and then I find some quiet nook where I can watch the terns dive after the whitebait, and the herring-gulls float without effort on the tides of the air.

Sometimes I hear the cry of the kittiwake. Then for a time I am far away from the surging crowd. I am on the cliffs of Ailsa Craig and hear again the chant of the gannets and the nursery cries of the nesting kittiwakes. The children play about me, the bathers may scream and laugh to their hearts' content. But my inner self is wandering amidst the places where the foot of man seldom treads.

The Early Morning Hours

I can truthfully say that there are very few people whom I really envy. There is, however, one class that stirs up this emotion. They are those who with rejoicing say: "The very moment I lay my head down on the pillow, I am off." I look at them wonderingly, enviously. Through storms, noise of traffic, worries, the buzz of conversations, sermons, they can sleep. Life yields to them her soporifics with a generous hand.

I, however, have never quite grown up. I must still have my lullaby. Here in the tent, wind and water are my best friends. Snuggling down between the blankets, I hear by the regular breathing of the other occupants that they are in Elysian fields. Sometimes I almost yield to the impulse of rousing them, just to let them know that I am still awake. But I refrain because such actions do not bring the best out of them.

Then I lie and listen. There is a slight movement of the tent. It lifts and swells with delight. The outermost leaves of the pear and plum branches begin to rustle with delicious movement, until the whole tree purrs at the stroking of the night breeze, which seems to slip away through a gap in the hedge, perchance to caress other favourites.

Meanwhile, the river tinkles on. It trips over the boulders which strew its path, and laughs as it spills itself into the main channel. It finds that it is faced with a great wall of sheer rock, and, after hurling itself in vain at this mighty fortress, glides with a chuckle around its base. But the music of both trees and river is born of resistance. Branches and rocks stand up to a great invisible power, and lo! the melody of effort sings in the night. And the moral is — But before I reach this strand of thought, I, too, am in the rounded arms of Lethe.

But if I am half-awake when I sleep, I am thankful to say that I am wide-awake as soon as I open my eyes. My companions, to use the language of cars, are cold starters. They need copious draughts of hot tea to warm them up before they can proceed in high gear. I am ready for action the moment I open my eyes. This, too, has its drawbacks as well as its advantages.

I look at my watch. It is 4.30a.m. I poke my head outside the tent and see the pearly light of another day creeping over the top of the eastern ridges. Not many living things are yet astir. The night prowlers, of course, will be thinking of screening themselves from inquisitive day.

But the robin and the flycatcher which nests in a tree by the tent are up and about. The former is piping away in a hedge which he is claiming as his own domain. How plaintive and yet how courageous is his song! In it are all the joyous strains of spring, yet the knowledge that autumn is coming, and after it the winter rigour,

169

sobers the carefree lilt of the earlier months, and his song is not always in a major key.

The flycatcher has a late brood of youngsters still to equip and send out into the world before all the corn is stacked; otherwise — So she, too, is up early, swerving and looping-the-loop in mid-air in her efforts to provide her hungry family with insects which know every trick of the unseen currents.

Meanwhile, Raq watches me as I dress. He sleeps at the foot of my bed, and at night accompanies me into the tent. There, with half-shut, almost apologetic eyes, he watches me undress. Never by any chance does he settle down to sleep until he sees me in bed. This is not merely affection, but rather that he does not intend that I should slip out on some night expedition without him.

Before I extinguish the light he comes up to me, receives his last caress, sniffs carefully to see that I really am tucked away, and then, having curled round once or twice, gives a big sigh that the joys of day are over, and sinks to rest on one of my old coats. Awake or asleep, he belongs to me.

Whilst dressing I have been turning over in my mind how I shall employ the early morning hours. Shall it be up the river with the clear-water worm, which, as all anglers know, is a deadly bait for trout if cast with care and skill? Or shall it be a mushroom hunt? The vision of those dainty ivory parasols with their pink under-lining decides for me what I shall do. This is one of the great joys of camping — the finding of your own food, food which is fresh from Nature's larder.

But first of all I arm myself with a hefty sandwich, and, calling Raq to heel, set off for my morning newspaper, which John Fell taught me to read. This, I hasten to say, is not one of those printed horrors which insure you for everything except the peril of reading and believing it. Mine lies alongside of the river — a little sandy bay with a surface which I smooth over night and morning, and which I visit when stars begin to peep at twilight, and pale before the glories of the morning sun.

As I glance at it I can see that I have had some visitors during the night. First of all, quite a big family of rats have passed that way in their nightly prowl for garbage. I follow the hand-like marks, and note how suddenly the raiders broke their leisurely formation and scampered hurriedly up the bank, kicking up the sand behind them. I look round for the cause of this sudden decision to retreat, and see no other mark on the sand which tells of the coming of some feared foe.

"I guess that owl we heard hooting last night has something to do with their commotion," I say to the dog, who is watching me from the grass. His tail gives a confirmatory wag.

In the far corner of the bay stands out a track which always thrills me — the five-toed mark of the otter.

"Passed by here not very long ago," I say to Raq. "The water is still oozing into the tracks."

I make a movement with my arm, and in a moment the spaniel has his nose down to the otter's signature.

171

"Seek," I say encouragingly; "good dog'; and away goes my companion along the underside of the bank.

"Steady," I call, as his eagerness takes him well away in front.

Through the shallows I plough my way, to find the dog standing over something which is shining like a silver crescent on the rocks. It is the otter's kill — a three-pound sea-trout, fresh up from the sea, his scales moonshine, shaded with the green depths of the ocean.

I pick up the fish, noting how that furred angler has taken a clean bite out of the shoulder. The rest of the fish is intact, and it goes into my pocket encased in a leaf of wild rhubarb.

"Make a nice breakfast for us," I say to Raq, who is  looking as pleased as Punch with himself. "A fish tastes as well caught by the otter as with a hook, only there is less of it."

One morning we found on our sandy newspaper the print of feet not unlike those of a sheep, only the stride was longer and there was a small indentation behind the deep grooves of the cloven hoofs.

We followed those tracks, summoning to our aid all the skill and caution of woodcraft that we knew. Like a wraith behind me stole my faithful follower, crouching when I laid myself flat, picking his way without sound, whilst his lolling tongue and sparkling eyes told of the keen enjoyment of the stalk.

After a mile of fatiguing, silent crawling, we had our reward, for below us in a quiet glade lay the wild deer whose imprints had lured us on. She was totally unaware of our presence, for the wind was kind to us and blew in our faces. For a moment or two we watched her as she inspected the great world around her by means of sensitive ears and nose. I gazed at those ears, fascinated by their beauty of movement and shape. One turned to the right, stayed there a moment, caught the sound which had caused it to veer; she said to herself, "Blackbird — no fear." Then the other pivoted round to the north, and the message was flashed down to her mind, "Bough creaking — no fear." Now she slightly lifted her gazelle-like head, and her nose became the ally of her ears. "Peat smoke — cottage on the hill — no fear." Then a blackberry-bush scratched itself against my cord knee-breeches. I only saw for a moment both her ears twitch round in my direction; whether she saw the gleam of my eyes or not I cannot say, for with a bound she was up and away, and I saw the white disc of her hindquarters fade to nothingness amidst the shadows of the hazel bushes.

"That was worth all the fag of trailing her," I said to Raq, and, after having a sniff at where she lay, he too cordially agreed with me. I thought he looked a trifle disappointed as he started to follow the trail she had left, and I called him to heel.

By this time I began to realize that the comfort of the early morning sandwich has worked itself out, and so I say to Raq, "Home, old man."

As we push our way through the wood almost every step entangles my face with unseen silken threads. "Gossamer," I murmur, and comfort myself with the reflection that this means fine weather, with no depression from Iceland looming in the offing.

Then down the lane, laden with honeysuckle and meadowsweet, we come to the caravan. Our little world is now astir. The cows at the farm have been turned out in the fields after milking; I can hear on the still air the "separator" buzzing out its great bee's drone. The calves standing at the gate can hear it too, and impatiently call for their morning meal. Somewhere a hen has managed to lay an egg, now that her moult is over; her pride in the achievement is manifest in her repeated clucking.

Both of us enter the camp with a cheery daylight-saving look on our faces.

"Breakfast ready?" I ask, as the smell of homefed ham stirs a welcome response within.

"Have you brought the water from the pump?" my wife counters, and I know that this is a gentle hint to remind me that "returning day brings new duties", and that "hallowed toil" and "consecrated labour" are things not merely to be sung about. Somehow or other they are beautiful ideas to linger over when accompanied on the organ and backed up by a good choir — but the pump is two hundred and fifty yards from the camp, and the way is steep, and the water is heavy, and the river may just be in fettle for the rod, and —

"Then there are the potatoes to peel," I hear her say again, "and we've only one loaf left."

"And the shop is two and a half miles away," comes a rather drowsy voice from the tent. "And it's my turn to go," continues my boy, cheering himself at the thought of it by whistling "It's a long way to Tipperary".

Then, after the ham, with its garlands of emerald watercress and its garnishing of mushrooms, has disappeared, we eagerly await the coming to the farm of the morning's post — not brought by old Ned — he is far away on his own rounds — but by a youth who leaves his cycle by the side of the pine wood that rims the broad highway nearly a mile and a half away.

Then I steal away with a belated newspaper, to read of the dizzy world I have left behind. Pleasure, money-making and money-worship, crime and divorce, meet the eyes on every page.

One begins to feel that life almost consists of these things when one peruses them within the roar of traffic and shut in with man-made streets. But, as I scan their often nauseating contents, I look up at the world at my feet — sunlight and shadow, swaying fields, the sweet smell of cattle as they browse in the meadow, Hermes shepherding the white flocks across the blue vault of heaven, the minnow leaping from his small pool for sheer joy of life, bees flying homewards rich with golden argosies — I know that what we read of in the papers are the world's excrescences, its deadly cankerous growths. The sweet, simple health of life lies before me — to be had for the asking, without money and without price.

I close the paper and return to camp to take up the pail which has the potatoes in it. There is a pleasure in scraping new tubers, even though the river is calling you. But there is still more pleasure in eating them — especially with the knowledge that you have dug them from the garden and scraped them ready for the table. There is pleasure, too, in eating mushrooms — still more if you have found the mushrooms yourself. I wonder whether one's dividend of pleasure is dependent on the capital of one's labour. Yes, I am still wondering — potatoes, mushrooms, scraping, finding — labour, delight.

The Covey

"I don't think Raq is very well this morning," I said to my wife, allowing at the same time a deep concern to creep into my tone. "His nose is warm and dry. I'll take him for a walk, I think."

"I hope you will enjoy it," she said, not looking at me.

"It was Raq I was thinking of," I said, with a sidelong glance.

"Of course," she murmured quietly — too quietly. Then she laughed and said, "Go and get your old brown suit on, dear. I've seen this coming on for over a week, and, when once the wandering fit is on you, there is only one cure."

"But Raq is —" I persisted.

"Waiting for you," she interrupted. "Look at his tail."

"That isn't the end by which you judge a dog's state of health. The tail —"

"Hasn't half been told," she said, beginning to make some sandwiches.

A few moments later the dog and I were on our way for an outing. I stooped down and felt his nose, just to make sure that the trip was thoroughly justifiable. It *was* a trifle warm. And so, with that contented feeling with which a Sabbatarian sets off in his car on Sunday

177

to visit a sick friend who resides in distant beautiful country, we set out.

At every turn of the road the dog looked round to see which way I intended to travel. When I turned into a certain lane, I believe he knew that we were bound for John Fell's estate, for he gave a short, snappy bark of delight, as though he knew the joys of scent and hunt which awaited him there.

Within an hour we were walking on the path which leads to the gamekeeper's hut. A dog's memory for many things is a wonderful storing-house. I noticed that he paused at bushes and carefully "winded" certain tufts of grass. Sometimes he poked his nose into their centre, and his tail for a second wagged furiously. Then he would turn and look at me for a moment, and I caught the flash of the whites of his eyes and the roguish look in them.

Then I too remembered that on other occasions he had, in every one of the places at which he had paused, found something of interest. In one he had flushed a woodcock, at another he had found a rat, whilst at a certain place in the hedge he had indicated to me that *something* was there. That something proved to be a hedgehog, curled up in dried leaves.

"Good dorg," I said to him, quietly, and encouragingly. Curious, how I always call him "dorg," not "dog," when I want him to hunt with care. I think it sounds more of a caress and less of a command.

As we neared the hut I called him to heel, and there we found John Fell having a quiet smoke. He was seated on a log, and might never have moved since our last visit.

"I've bin thinking of ye," was his greeting to me, as the dog rushed forward and fondled him. "Just a bit out o' sorts he is too," continued the keeper, putting his hand on Raq's nose.

"Thank you, John," said I heartily.

"What for?" said he quickly.

"Oh, nothing in particular," I answered thoughtfully.

When I had seated myself I said:

"And how's the partridges and pheasants getting on? Getting good bags?"

John shook his head ruefully.

"Pheasants not too bad — partridge nothing. Hardly a good covey about the place — young birds scarce as elephants — never known such a bad season for 'ears."

"One of my favourite birds is the partridge," said I, wondering whether he could be drawn.

"Same 'ere," said he readily. "Has a family life, too, that makes me sorry they have to be shot. Cock and hen make good parents — not beaten even by the otter."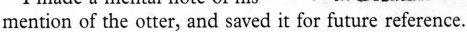

I made a mental note of his mention of the otter, and saved it for future reference.

"Ever seen 'er do the broken-wing trick when she has her 'cheepers' round her?" said he, his face expanding into a pleasant smile as he thought of the bird's wiliness.

I nodded. I was very familiar with it. So was Raq.

"Seen the vanishing trick as well?" he asked.

179

"Never," I said, hoping my answer sounded truthful, for I delighted in hearing him forget his reserve as he described his favourites.

"Well, that's worth seein'," he continued. "Many a time I've got quietly over a stile and found myself right in the midst of the two old birds and a dozen youngsters. Most of 'em glide into the hedge like silk. Then ye walk carefully, for ye know that somewhere by yer feet two or three will be lyin' doggo.

"After a minute or two, ye pick 'em out; ye'd think they were little bits o' muck with shadders on 'em. They lie without breathin', only their bright beads of eyes shinin' like jet. Then, from one o' the bushes, out flies the cock with such a fuss and a whirr of his wings that ye are startled. Away he goes ower the hedge and into the next field. Only fer a second do ye foller him with yer eyes. Then ye turn to the little beggars at yer feet."

"Well?" I asked breathlessly.

"They're not there," said the keeper, with a broad grin of satisfaction. "Ye've bin done brown. The moment the old bird spluttered out o' the bushes those innercent youngsters bolted into the hedge liked greased lightning; ye only needed to look away for a second fer 'em to take the chance. The old cock gave 'em their chance, and they took it."

John chuckled with delight at his memories, and told me that not once but scores of times he had been deceived like that.

"Then, o' course," he continued, "the whole family would come together to a place where the mother called fer 'em — like this," he said, and, blowing through his empty pipe, he emulated the call so perfectly that Raq leapt to his feet and, putting his nose up, tried to catch the scent of the birds he felt sure were near.

"He's a right 'un is that dog of yourn," said John warmly, whilst I glowed with pride to hear such praise of my beloved companion. Strange how a man never likes to hear his own wife praised in his presence, probably on the principle that good wine needs no bush; but there is nothing better than to have your dog rightly appraised.

"You said something about liking the family life of the partridge," I said.

"That's right," he said. "Would you believe it, I have known when the eggs has bin hatchin' under the hen, fer the cock to take the earliest out and dry 'em with his own 'eat, whilst she was busy bringing the rest out. She kept sittin' on the nest, and as soon as the little beggars could struggle on to their legs — they went to father until their brothers and sisters were out o' the shell. That's what I call family life, that is."

He paused for a moment, and I ventured to remark:

"That is real equality of the sexes — both for pleasure and for responsibility."

"That about hits it off," said John. "And then, right through the weeks that foller, ye can see the two on 'em with their little brood growin' up around 'em; and, if they weren't shot, I reckon they'd all stay together till the spring come round."

"And the pheasant?" I asked.

181

John made a motion of disgust.

"A sort of hireling husband," he said, "always thinking of his own skin — safety first is his motter. I shed no tears when I see a rocketing cock spiral down as dead as a stone."

He looked at his watch.

"Well," he said, "I must be off."

"What are you busy with now?" I asked.

"Oh, keepin' the rabbits down — snares, ye know — 'gins', some folks call 'em. Don't like it, poor little beggars, but it's got to be done; they do such a 'eap o' damage."

"I'll keep you company part of the way," I said.

I motioned to Raq with my arm, and he ran ahead a few yards, keeping, like the wise dog he was, on the lee side, so that the breeze would waft any interesting scent to him.

"Hear that bird follerin' and hollerin' at him?" asked my companion.

"A wren," I answered, "treating him as she would a fox."

"You're right," he replied. "And there's another instance o' family life."

We walked on in silence, and I knew that he would choose his own time to explain his last statement.

Soon we came to a tree thickly overgrown with ivy, and here John halted. In the roots of the ivy which criss-crossed the trunk was a domed nest made of moss, with a small hole for an entrance.

"Feel in it," said John, and, having done so, we walked on a few yards.

Here he pointed to a similar nest built under an overhanging bank, and he motioned me to put my fingers again inside.

"Any difference?" he asked in his usual abrupt way.

"First was unlined, second one lined with feathers," I said.

"That's due to family instincts," he explained. "The wrens build several roosts, but the eggs are laid in the feather-lined nest. When the hen is sitting, the cock retires to roost into one of the other apartments. And when the youngsters are hatched, the family doesn't lose touch with one another, like the thrush or the blackbird. They keep together and cuddle up at night in one of their country residences."

Before we parted, John pointed out to me a sparrowhawk seated on a bare branch at the side of a wood. It vanished like a streak of grey-blue smoke.

"There's another kind o' family life with those killers," he said. "The hen is bigger than the cock. Nearly all the hawks are like that. There's the peregrine falcon, for instance."

"Why do you think that is?" I asked.

He chuckled.

"I rather think that if I was a female hawk, and had a husband with his instincts, I should want to be bigger than him. Mind ye," here he turned and looked at me, "it's only my way o' thinkin', but if he should see red some day when 'is own nestlings are in the fork of a tree, it's well fer them that there should be a big mother handy."

We parted at the lane which led to his house. He had asked me to come in and "have a bite o' dinner," and when I replied, "No, thank you; I can have a meal indoors any day," he had smiled and understood.

On my way home I was busy with the gamekeeper's facts. Big families seemed to lead to closer family life. There were the tits and the ducks — all proud possessors of a numerous progeny. But, then, there rose before me the pheasant and the rabbit, and, when I thought of the insect world also, then my inferences were dashed to pieces.

So I turned to the keeper's choice of words which distinguished the permanent from the temporary residences of the wren — a nest and a roost.

I could see in imagination the little bird settling down on her eggs or youngsters with a sigh of relief, pleasure, satisfaction, after the toils of the day. It spoke to me of moorages, anchorages, foundations.

Then I thought of the roosts — and the former images of restfulness were displaced by others which reminded me of change, fitfulness, itinerancy.

I rather fancy that many modern residences are merely private hotels — roosts for the dark hours, but not homes. And as I entered my own dwelling there were two verses which hovered about my thoughts — "Abide in Me" — therein is the permanent nest. And, as a background to it, "As a bird that wandereth from her nest, so is a man that wandereth from his place".

The Lure of the River

I have always thought that it must be a difficult matter to furnish and stock a shop so that it is at once attractive and yet not too smart.

There are many establishments which, by their very ornateness, make one feel that nothing but an order for a suite of furniture will be considered or will be welcome. One enters such places and asks for a couple of yards of webbing in the tone of voice that one would use on entering Claridge's and asking for a poached egg.

But John Rubb's shop is not of these.

It is the resort of farmers, gardeners, anglers, and devotees of the great god Sport, and those who dwell in the quiet places of the hills enter and feel at home. John is not only a salesman; he is an adviser, a recommender.

True, he will usually recommend the choosing of the dearer article. But then, well, he knows that, in the long run, cheapness is not economy.

"That will be two pounds fifteen" — then follows the slightest of pauses and a slight dropping of the voice — "*to you*," he says to a farmer who has entered the shop determined not to spend more than two pounds on a mackintosh. It is the friendly accent on the "to you" that usually wins the day. "Concession is the maker of profits," is one of John's mottoes.

"No," says he to an angler who has turned the fifties, "those waders you have in your hand are good, but they are not thick enough *for you*. Right enough for a young fellow in his teens — they can stand the cold water. But you need to keep warm." Needless to say, the better waders are chosen, and rightly so.

Many times have I seen my friend stand watching the rising trout. I have been as keen as mustard to start at once, and chided him for his slowness in making a beginning. But he was investigating what flies the fish were rising to, noticing what part of the flats or streams they had a predilection for. Then would come the search in his fly-book for the nearest imitation to the real.

"Business," he would say when I chaffed him about some of his customers, "is like fly-fishing. You must study appetites. No good casting a Wickam's Fancy if they're feedin' on the Stone Fly."

Once, after I had flogged the water for the whole day and had practically an empty creel, I found that he had a good basket of fish.

"What fly did you tie on?" I asked.

He smiled, and replied, "I never got a touch with the fly, but I noticed trout feedin' under the alder and willow bushes. They were sucking in the caterpillars which fell off the leaves."

"And so you collected a few and used them as bait?" I said.

186

"Forcible feedin' ain't no use in the stream," he said. "Find out what the fish are after. Go to any trouble. It pays — in business, in sport" — here he paused deliberately, and added significantly — "in any profession."

He finished by saying quietly: "And, remember, the real beats the artificial bait — every time."

So into this homely establishment I walked one morning.

"Well," said John, looking out at me through spectacles which narrowed but could not destroy the kindly gleam of his eyes.

"The sea-trout are up," said I. Such a pronouncement I knew was the best bait I could throw.

"And when is it to be?" he answered immediately.

"What about to-night?" I asked, carrying out a motto of "Do it now" which hangs in my study.

And so, later in the day, just to be in time for the early rise, John and I set off in the old Ford.

As Raq jumped in with us John said:

"That dog of yours can do nearly anything. Pity he can't scent out the big fish like he can the pheasants."

I wish I could describe the river at which we finally arrived. Before we plunged down the valley to its banks we could hear the murmur of its running waters, like the sibilant whisperings of some distant crowd. As we approached, so the individual voices could be distinguished. There was the laughter of the fast stream as it hurried over jewelled stones. How beautiful everything submerged in water appears! A bit of

187

bottle-glass gleams like an emerald, a broken flower-pot burns red like a ruby. Amethyst, amber, topaz, beryl, sapphire, shone beneath the polish of the running wavelets.

We sat for some time drinking in the beauty of it all.

"It's the accessories of angling which are so good," whispered my companion, "even if you never get a single fish."

There was no need to answer. We both felt the all-pervasive loveliness.

Looking away to the right, we could see and follow the course of the waters as they meandered through their highway. In the shade of the distant pines lay the Dormant — the sleeping pool, whose dark depths were reported to be unfathomable. There the salmon took rest after facing the flood which had lured them from the estuary. Nearer to us lay "Clinty the glittering", disappointing ever from an angler's point of view. Nearer still spread out "Blaney", so called because it was the favourite haunt of one who has gone, and where I hauled into the net my first sea-trout, whilst John quietly watched with critical eyes the tactics and strategy of his pupil.

"There's a good trout rising in that pool there," said my companion, pointing to quieter waters which lay at our feet. I looked, and saw the fairy ring with its dimpled centre which thrills every angler's heart.

"How do you know it was a trout and not a 'skelly'?" I asked. "Skelly," I may say, is the term used for all fish that are not of the trout variety. It is a term of reproach. One thinks (at least in this district) of a "skelly" fisher as one thinks of a man who, in billiards, continually "pots" his opponent's white ball. The thing's not done.

"A skelly, when it rises," said John, "leaves behind it, in the ring which it makes, a big bubble of air. You can hear the big chub suckin' like young pigs sometimes. But let's go down to the bridge yonder and look at the water. It's too early to start fishing yet."

And so we came to the bridge, and, lying full length, with our heads just over the edge, we gazed into the moving waters.

"I wonder how those beetles manage to skim along on the top of the pools," I said, indicating little black dots of life which moved in the quiet backwaters.

"Ever heard of the surface-film?" asked my companion.

I shook my head.

"Ever made a needle float in a basin of water?" John asked.

"When I was a boy — many a time," I replied.

"How is it, then, that 'the iron did swim'?" he asked. Then, answering his own question, he went on, "The top of the water is in a state of tension — stretched tight like elastic. So long as anything doesn't burst through the film, even though it's heavier than the water, it'll float all right. Those beetles have got on their feet what I call 'skis' — they spread out on the top — that's why they can skim about. But look carefully beneath you."

I looked into the water beneath the bridge.

"See that dark shadow there?" said John, pointing carefully. "He's a pounder if he's an ounce. He's the head man of this trout community under the bridge here. Look carefully and you'll see his neighbours."

After my eyes had grown accustomed to the lights and shadows, I began to pick out other forms.

"You'll notice he's got the best position for food," said John. "See how the stream swings the major portion of anything that is in the river towards where he lies — that is the coveted position. He holds that vantage-point by the might of his sharp teeth. See that?" he asked.

One of the other trout, not so large as the chieftain, but bigger than the rest, had approached nearer to the pounder's lair than was good for his health. Like a flash the big trout had dashed at him, and quicker than a flash the other had vanished. He had no wish for a gashed side.

"Every trout has its chosen position," John went on. "The big ones pick the main food highways. Then the others, all according to their strength, wait in the byways for the crumbs which fall from the rich man's table. If I caught the chief to-night, the next in strength would step into his place, and all the rest would similarly move up."

As the sun sank to rest, John and I parted, agreeing to fish separately, but making a rendezvous at an appointed time.

"Remember," he said to me as a parting word of advice, "the one universal rule of good angling: Keep out of sight — keep more out of sight — then keep more out of sight than ever."

And so I took up a stance where the stream ran into a quieter pool. On the side opposite to me the pines

190

frowned down on deeper water, and the alder bushes and willows screened the bank. Behind me lay a bed of shingle, and then the land rose like a cliff where bushes and ferns had found precarious foothold.

Slowly the daylight faded. The rooks wheeled homewards, the wood-pigeons sought the quiet sanctuaries of the woods. Trees began to lose their sharp outlines, the curlew's pipe echoed above the ripple of the stream, and the snipe drummed out his love in circles of dashing flight.

I had netted a couple of yellow trout when, in the tree quite close to me, I heard a sound like the whine of young pups. Farther off there floated on the air a long quavering "Hoo-hoo-hoo-oo-oo."

I looked up, and I could just discern two young brown owls. They had come as quietly as wraiths. Theirs was the whining cry. The long "Hoo" was the answer of the parent bird.

Soon she comes with noiseless flight — not a wing-beat is distinguishable. She settles on a bare branch which overhangs the river, and I can just discern the heads of the young owlets turned expectantly towards her.

In the shallows below the older bird there is movement. Once I thought I could discern the flash of silver scales as a fish turned on its side in the water. From the bare branch a brown body drops like a stone. There is a rush of startled fish from the shallows. Two or three leap high out of the water in

191

their frantic endeavour to reach the darker protecting depths. But the mother owl is on the bank holding a half-pounder in her talons. I can see the gleam in those great glowing orbs which miss nothing in the gathering darkness. A flapping of wings above me, and more whines, tell me that the young owlets are enjoying their first course. A little later the *entrée* will consist of mice and a rat or two. They will account for the best part of a score before the dawn sends them home.

Now warm night has indeed taken possession. All sounds seem to take on a different tone from the day. I am fishing in the quieter, shallower water, for big fish emerge out of the depths and seek their food nearer the banks at night.

Somewhere in the darkness I can hear the cattle nipping off the grass in the meadows. Above me a couple of wild duck speed with whistling wings, whilst further up the river I hear the metallic clank of the heron's raucous call.

Such sounds intrigue me even more than the catching of fish. I love to watch the shadows move, and to see the tangle of rushes and weeds by the bank stir restlessly, to listen to the sedge-warbler's midnight chatter, and to hear the tree-tops move ever so slightly in the cool air which plays amongst them. I can hear them sigh out their quiet enjoyment. And underneath every sound is the ripple-ripple-ripple of the stream, changing its rhythm every few moments: Ripple, ripple — Ripple; ripple — Ripple, ripple; ripple — Ripple — ripple.

I found John later sitting on the bank puffing at his pipe.

"Had any luck?" I asked.

"Never a fish," said he; "but, man, what a night!

"There is a river the streams whereof make glad the city of God," murmured my companion, as we set our faces once more towards the city of man.

A Triumph of Training

Three times in the year our house passes through a minor crisis. Towards the end of January, April, and September, certain symptoms manifest themselves in my wife's demeanour: I find her a trifle distrait, and catch her looking rather critically at my boy, who is growing rapidly.

At these times she spends a good deal of her time on her knees, and, lest I should create a wrong impression, I hasten to say that before her lies an open trunk.

"One on his back, one on the kitchen airer, one to be mended, and one in the box," I hear her murmur, as she gazes at a printed form which is called an "inventory".

Then I know it is time for my boy to return to school, and that it is useless to plan an outing with her — she is thinking in terms of shirts, socks, handkerchiefs, boots. He is thinking too, but in quite other terms.

I occupy the place of consultant expert on questions which I know my wife has already made up her mind about. He is called in to parade in full and undress uniform, in order that we may see whether there are any surplus hems to his clothes which may be let down in view of his growing capacities. Unfortunately my small family is not graded very well — there is no Tommy and Dick who can wear the mantle discarded by the eldest.

Whilst I do my bit in making indelible blots with indelible ink on the inaccessible parts of stiff Sabbatic collars, I hear a conversation going on in the front bedroom. It is disconnected because both are intent on different boxes.

"I've packed your handkerchiefs, socks, boots, and —"

"You won't forget the raspberry jam you promised, will you, Mother?"

"Will you need this coat this term or —"

"Yes, Mother, and tinned peaches I like better than apricots."

"This pair of socks and these cricket shirts don't belong to you — they must belong to some other boy, so when you get back see that you —"

"Yes, Mother, and that chicken-and-ham paste which you put in last term was topping."

It is at this stage that I think it fitting to intervene, and in the midst of my ink-splashing I call out sternly:

"Listen to what your mother is saying, and take a bit of interest in the packing of your things."

"All right, Dad," comes the reply; "but have you marked my fives gloves and footer boots yet?"

Personally I think that matters would be simplified if for the last week of the holidays a boy were kept in bed. All mending, washing, darning, adjusting could then be carried out at leisure.

And so the cyclone envelops us and the whole house revolves round a big box, a "tuck" box, and an attendant attaché-case.

With a sigh of relief I finally hear myself called to strap the trunk. Like a skilful porter I steer it downstairs. Boxes are never by any chance packed downstairs. They are made as heavy as possible in the bedroom before they are ready for the hall.

Having asked my wife in my most willing-to-help tone whether there was anything more that I could do, and having been assured in a tone which was really grateful, but implied that my absence for a few hours would be still more appreciated, with the light heart which comes to those who have nobly done their duty, I called to Raq, and soon we were in the misty fields.

Up the hedges we tramped, where the blackberries were hanging in thick clusters, and where the goldfinches fluttered from the thistle plumes, like golden drops spurting from some living fountain.

A light breeze blew steadily over the fields of corn, drying and ripening the stooks of oats not yet stacked. From these the birds took their toll, storing up in their little bodies the energy which stands them in good stead when winter brings the hunger moon.

In the distance I heard a jolly voice singing, "Oh, who will o'er the downs with me", and, recognizing the tones of that beloved vagabond, Jerry, we hastened until we came across him in the lane.

"Having a day off?" I said, with that slight touch of friendly sarcasm with which I always greet him.

196

"If you only knew how hard at it I've bin since I last saw yer, you'd spend yer time urgin' me not to overdo it," he answered, with that disarming smile of his. "Just goin' down by the river," he said.

"So the salmon are up, are they?" I said.

"A fine run came up with the last flood," he answered, "and I'm a-goin' to feast my eyes on 'em."

I looked at the long ash stick he carried.

"Too long for walking with, Jerry," I said. "Let your eyes be the only things that feast," I added warningly.

Together we walked down to the rippling waters. There is no one that I delight to walk with more than Jerry. Give me Ned for whimsicality and John Fell for soundness, but let me have Jerry for sheer woodcraft and for insight into the mind of the little people of the fields.

He pointed out to me the nest of the dipper, domed and like a monster wren's, wedged in the crevice of the rocks, its roof protecting it from the spray of the small waterfall that splashed near.

"And there's the owner of it, I'll be bound," he said, as we looked at a rotund, cubby bird, with the body of a blackbird and a tail three sizes too small for its plump roundness.  "Look at the crescent moon underneath its throat," he added, "and watch it bobbing up and down in an absent-minded kind o' way."

"Looks as though it's spent its life in the country, and carries on the old custom of curtsying," I said.

"Ye've hit it fine," he said appreciatively. "That there bird never leaves its river. It never seems to have noticed modern ways, but sticks to its own little bit o' country, and in consequence its manners are them o' the Middle Ages."

We watched it for a moment as it plunged underneath the sparkling waters, quietly emerging to take up its curtsying stance in a smooth backwater.

"Think on't," he added. "Natur' meant that bird to live on the land. But away back, perhaps thousands o' years ago, it suddenly made up its mind that a duck's life were better'n a dipper's. So bit by bit it got more used to th' watter, till finally it flies where the duck dives."

"Flies?" I said, incredulously.

"Aye," said Jerry, "I said 'flies'."

We posted ourselves on a small bridge, and the bird obliged us by taking to the crystal water. Then we could see that, once submerged, it did not walk on the gravelly bottom, but used its wings in a similar manner to what it does when in the air.

I looked at my companion with wonder in my eyes.

"Fancy a thrush trying to do that," he said, with profound satisfaction.

Then, turning to me, he asked suddenly:

"How would you like to live on bird-seed from now on?"

"It's about all that is left to us," I said, thinking of the curtailment of our menus which diet experts are now urging upon us; and then I added, "It would be a rather drastic change, though."

Jerry nodded. "But that's what the dipper has done. He's left the fields' larder and turned to what the river stores up — cultivated a new taste and a new appetite, and searches for it in the shadowy watters, not in the sunlit medders. His little white crescent gleams like a lighthouse i' the dark."

As we walked on by the gliding stream he continued:

"But think what trouble those birds have in educatin' their youngsters up to it! Think —"

But Jerry's words had touched a certain inner trigger and released certain inner emotions which I thought I had left at home. Perhaps it was that phrase of his, "Educatin' their youngsters", which made me interrupt him and ask:

"Ever seen an inventory?"

"Can't say as ever I 'ave," he answered doubtfully. "Is it the workshop of an inventor?"

"No," I said, smiling in spite of myself, at the same time seeing in my mind a list which ran, "Suits of clothes, overcoats, mackintosh, rug, dressing-gown, flannel shirts, white shirts, night-shirts or pyjamas, summer vests, collars, socks, summer and winter pants (must be worn), handkerchiefs, ties, towels, brushes, bags, sheets, boots, shoes, slippers, football and cricket boots, football and cricket jerseys" . . . "No," I said, "it's not the workshop of an inventor, though sometimes I rather fancy it's the work of one. But go on with what you were saying about education and the dipper."

"Well," said he, a trifle mystified by my interruption, "when a young bird is hatched oot, it comes into the

199

world with a taste fer the things which Natur' designed it to 'ave."

"You mean," I said, "that a thrush is born with a natural craving for flies, caterpillars, worms, and snails?"

"Aye," said my companion, "that's the nateral way o' things. And the young dippers come oot wi' a taste for a land diet, and when they grow up a bit they have a likin' fer flittin' aboot the bushes and the fields."

He paused to look hard at me to see whether I could now "carry on" the problem which confronts the adult birds.

"You mean, I take it," I said, "that the young birds shout for meat, and the parent birds come to them, so to speak, with fish."

"Well," said Jerry, gratified that I had grasped the essentials, "that's near enough, anyhow. And it may be that them dippers at first may give 'em a few flies, &c. Then they start educatin' 'em to river food, and the taste fer that is to the young dippers what termatoes and gorgonzoli cheese is to us — it 'as to be cultivated.

"But" — here he looked round, and with a sweep of his arm embraced a wide terrain — "what I'm sayin' about these birds might be said a'most of all wild things. If there's no educatin' of 'em they soon snuff out."

I refrained from making any comment, for I could see he was anxious to proceed.

"Otters have to train their youngsters how to catch fish and eat it. Foxes bring home dead rabbits and teach the little 'uns how to eat it and how to hide what they don't want. Thrushes and blackbirds train their little 'uns to crouch, to stand still as death. Were there no schools for wild Natur's childer, most on 'em would never grow up — they'd all die early, untimely deaths. Those which do the most in educatin' their young have the satisfaction of addin' perhaps years to their lives."

We had now reached a part of the river where quiet pools lay between brawling streams, and, knowing that Jerry would like to prowl along unfettered by a companion, we left him — with his ash stick.

"Don't fergit," were his parting words to me, "when you see the dipper, think of the bravery which suddenly determined to make a living by divin' and swimmin' fer it — and without webbed feet or any sundry fittings fer such a life. And don't fergit," he added, "what a task it must be fer them old birds to indooce their land-lovin' youngsters to wet their black feathers in a threatenin' river — it's a triumph of patient schoolin'."

"And don't fergit," I mimicked him, "to keep that ash stick out of sight if you meet John Fell. He'll not mistake it for a walking-stick, I can tell you. He'll be diving into your pockets for the gaff."

As I returned home that last phrase of Jerry's hovered continually in my mind — "It's a triumph of patient schoolin'".

I thought of my own boy, typical of thousands of others, born with a natural taste for jam (by the pot,

201

not by the teaspoonful), peaches, cake, and every other deadly article of diet, but now returning to the simple fare of school life.

Also he will be confronted with Cicero and Sophocles. On his plate will be placed "maths" and history, whilst his real taste will hunger for the playing-field and its glories. The young dipper will be faced with a selection of things the taste for which will need careful cultivation.

If only these things turn him out as fit to face his world as the dipper faces his, "schoolin'" will have indeed achieved a triumph!

Labour-Saving

We have always been keen on labour-saving at our house. Until recently I have been quite as keen as my wife. It is only within the last few months that my zeal has somewhat abated — but I must not anticipate.

Referring to one or two things which we happen to possess, how often have I heard her say, "We have an electric-iron and a radiator, and if only we had a vacuum-cleaner I am sure I could do without a maid."

Of course, when she uttered such statements our maid was still with us. Her name was Emma. She herself was a labour-saver. The amount she could save herself from attempting in a single day was marvellous. We looked upon her as a fixture who moved when the furniture suffered the usual triennial upheaval.

But in the course of the twelve years that she clung to us she undoubtedly saved me from a good deal of routine, for during that time she developed almost an uncanny sense for anticipating callers' business.

To a young couple who stood shyly asking for the minister, she would say ingratiatingly, "And is it a weddin' that you've come about?" After the sweet young things had confessed that that was their business they felt perfectly at ease — the great bogey of beginning to explain their errand had lost its terrors.

If, however, the caller came about a funeral, Emma sensed it at once. For all tragedy and morbidness she had the nose of Raq. Assuming her most downcast and dejected air, she would show the mourner into the lounge as though she were ushering him into a morgue.

She took rather longer to learn the ways of the various "mouchers" and beggars who think every minister is fair game. But at last she grew quite expert in discrimination. Only once did she make a mistake that mattered. But then it was the trustee's own fault by appearing so slatternly in public.

Now Emma has departed, and in her place stands a vacuum-cleaner. With the nozzle in her hand, my wife sounds like some giant bee as she sucks the dust from easy and remote corners. Raq's coat is cleaned by it. Instead of the usual hand-brush, the clothes I stand up in are subjected to its searching suction. In my den, microscopic specimens which I have collected with great care vanish up its relentless gullet.

The principle might be extended with advantage, I think, to our churches. Collection-boxes in time might disappear, and a really powerful, silent suction, held at the pew-end, might draw from small-necked pockets a fair yield in loose cash.

It was a real summer's day when Raq and I reached the farm. There was no need to ask what the immediate task of the workers might be. Every lane was littered with wisps of dry grass, and the overhanging branches of the trees were pennoned with the hay filched from the rolling wains as they lurched towards the farm.

We found Joe and Alan busy building a huge stack. The former was on the top, receiving the loads which his brother lifted dexterously by means of a long-handled pitch-fork.

I watched them for a time, and then, by way of drawing them out, said:

"There's an art in building a stack."

"Ye're right there," said Alan, standing in the empty cart. "Ye mun keep the sides plumb or ye'll have trouble when the winds play roond it."

"Aye," said Joe, "and ye mun distribute the hay evenly and tread it doon."

"It looks to me a trifle higher in the centre than the sides," I said critically.

"That's as it should be," said Joe. "If it were 'oller in t' centre any damp or rain that got in would run to t' middle — then there'd be rot to deal with."

"Or it might fire of itsen," added his brother.

In a moment or two both of them descended. The empty cart rumbled upwards toward the High Barn, and, whilst a full one waited, we all of us sought the shade and had a modified "ten o'clock."

Wonderfully peaceful was the sight before us. The sky was cloudless. Immensity robed itself in blue, the colour of hope. The land shimmered under the burning heat. Swallows and swifts hawked the higher air. The horse, resting with its heavy load, used its tail as a whisk, and wrinkled up the skin on its shining coat to displace the fly assemblies that held their meetings there.

"Wish I could crinkle up the skin on my face like that old horse," said Alan; "it 'ud save a mighty lot of hand-waggin' — pesty things these flies."

I turned towards Joe as Alan spoke, for I had a dim recollection of seeing him do something which, at the time, set me thinking.

"Take your cap off a minute, will you?" I asked.

Joe complied.

"Now," I said, "raise your eyebrows and forehead up and down quickly."

He did so, and, as he performed, I touched Alan's arm and pointed to the top of his brother's scalp.

"It's movin'," said he.

Joe put his hand up to his own head.

"It's doin' more'n that," he said; "it's crinklin' up like a small concertina."

"Like that owd 'orse," added his brother, nodding at Beauty.

I smiled, but said nothing. Both of them knew what I was trying to point out.

"I can't do it," said Alan, puckering up his eyebrows in vain.

"Too thick a skin," said Joe, with a grin.

"You're nearer the animal," said Alan, nudging him.

For a moment or two Joe continued his experiments. Alan watched him closely. "Well, I'm blessed," he added, "his ears are movin' too."

Before Joe could reply, I said, "It would save a lot of labour if those muscles of his were as strong as they were in all of us once upon a time, perhaps hundreds of thousands of years ago."

"Aye," said Alan, with a coaxing inflexion that showed he was waiting for more information.

"There are in all of us," I continued, "the remnants of muscles which once were in full use and in full control. Look at old Beauty there," I said, pointing to the horse. "See how she swings her ears, turns them backwards, sideways, or forrards." I paused a moment and then added, "We could do that once. Joe's powers are a witness to the fact. We've lost control by not using them."

We were all silent for a time. I think we were looking down the long vista of the years — thinking perhaps of the pit out of which we have been dug.

Then Alan said:

"If I were you, Joe, I should give half an hour every morning to that ear-waggin' business. You'd save yoursel' no end o' labour in smackin' off t' flies from thi' face."

"What's Billy doing with the scythe?" I asked, as I saw one of their men making his way up a field with old Father Time's weapon slung over his shoulder. "You don't use a scythe nowadays, do you?"

"He's a-goin' to cut a way for t' mower. We begin on another field in the mornin'."

The sight of the scythe raised memories in my friends' minds, for Alan said, "My feyther minds the day when grass and corn were all cut by hand. Now everything is done by machinery."

"That's true," said Joe. "You can milk t' coos wi' a big sort o' vacuum-cleaner. You can separate t' milk by cogs and wheels. Tractors pull t' ploos (ploughs) and save the horses from hard work. Everything is being invented to save labour, and yet I don't know" — here he raised his cap and scratched his head — "I think we have to work as hard as ever."

"I don't think we do," said Alan. "Our days are not so long. Now we can get a few hours off, and t' collar-work isn't as stiff as it was." He paused a moment and continued: "I've heerd my feyther tell of the hay harvest when he were in his young days. Then the farm hands stood in line, the scythes in their hands, ready to take their time from the leading 'stroke'. In them days they worked from the crowin' o' the cock till the stars appeared. For a whole corn harvest a man could earn aboot eight or nine pun, thatchin' included. They had to turn the hay by hand, bind the sheaves by hand, rake in the same way. Now we have the mower, the swathe-turner, the cutter and binder fer corn, and some have elevators to lift it. The new has displaced the old."

"And the old makes a way for the new," I said, thinking of the scythe, which was going to cut a clear margin for the "cutter" to work in. "As it should do — always," I added quietly.

"The time'll come," said Joe, "when to the binder which cuts the corn they'll fix a thresher, a grindin' mill, a kneader, and an oven heated wi' petrol. Then a sheaf'll go in at one end and come out a loaf o' bread at t' other."

"Like the pig in the American stock-yards," I said. "It enters a pig and comes out as sausage, everything being utilized except the squeal."

The brothers laughed, and one of them said, "We're gettin' a mechanized army. We shall get a mechanized life if we're not careful. Labour-savin' machines have their good points. The great trouble wi' 'em is that they make men lose their personal skill."

"What you don't use," said Alan, tapping Joe lightly on the crown of his head, "you lose."

After we had added the "vacuum" to our housekeeping implements, my wife and I went to an electrical exhibition. For my birthday I was going to be presented with an electrical hot-water apparatus to facilitate shaving.

Before we left I found myself, instead, the purchaser of an electric washing-machine. The difference that washer would make to our home-life, I was assured, would be marvellous. It certainly made a difference to my bank balance!

I came home with visions of all labour ended, my wife ready to go out with me whenever she desired it. The whole household would be pervaded with that "I'll mow that lawn to-morrow" feeling — buoyant, health-giving.

But I still hear a voice from the depths of the cellar saying, "Would you mind helping me to fold these sheets, dear?" I leave my books, and, with a sigh for

Emma, say, "But I thought that new washer did all this sort of thing."

As far as I can see, there still remain for us to purchase a bed-making machine and a mechanical washer-up.

I have hinted that Raq cleans plates in a really marvellous fashion. But I never got much further than the hint. Once when my wife and the whole family were down with the "flu" and I, even I only, was left to look after them, I found him very useful. I was never troubled with greasy water. But I must not enlarge on details, as I may be thought a workshirker, instead of which I wish to concentrate thought on the dog as a labour-saver.

Then I think we might go on to an electric cooker, bed-heater, and slot-machines for compressed tabloid foods of approved strength in vitamins. But the snag of all these things is that they are labour-saving to the housewife only.

Had I kept a diary of the past few weeks, many of my morning entries would have run thus:

Monday. — Electric-iron refused to electric. Hour spent in locating trouble. Two minutes spent in adjusting the terminals.

Tuesday. — Vacuum-cleaner went on strike. Having post-mortemed its inside, accidentally dropped it on the floor. Works started automatically. Nothing like firmness in dealing with a vacuum. Nature abhors one.

Wednesday. — All lights in the house fused or refused to give illumination on Tuesday night. Searched for cause of trouble in remote fuseboxes. Found it not. After a vain search for a lengthy period, saw men outside working on the main cable. Concluded the trouble was really there. Correct.

Thursday. — Wife complained of receiving a shock from wall-plug. Put it right in two minutes, but, as she offered to write my class-tickets whilst I was busy, took a long time over the job. First bit of luck labour-saving apparatus has brought me.

Monday. — Busy writing *Recorder* article. Washer refused to wash. Water boiling, clothes all ready, lovely drying day, wife slightly perturbed in manner with a tendency to irritability. After an hour's search found that she had overlooked the turning on of the switch.

Thus my enthusiasm for such things has received a slight setback. Labour-saving implements are all right, but they must be labour-saving not for some of the people all the time, nor for all the people some of the time, but for all the people and all the time.

On thinking things over I do not think we shall get the other inventions until the guarantee includes this.

A Spurt o' Furious Life

Many are the signs in field and wood that autumn has now definitely established itself. The grass is still emerald, the wood-pigeon still coos out an abbreviated, hyphenated love-song of a faithfulness which he never possesses, but the woods are comparatively silent.

As Raq and I travel through the fields we miss the little yellow-hammer's ode to warmth; the melodious hum of insect life has died down. Only the robin sings cheerily of the springs which are still to come, and tries to convince us that winter is but spring in the making.

Other signs there are, too, for those who can read them. Away in the distance we heard the boom of the guns, and knew that the advent of October meant death to the pheasants.

Now also are the finches gathering themselves into flocks. As we went along I counted sixteen goldfinches feeding on thistles. Very dainty they looked as they swayed on those bowing plumes. They were rather a snobbish little band, too, and drove away any other bird which encroached on their preserves.

For a moment or two I watched a pair of the older birds, the cock resplendent in scarlet head and his black wings striped with golden slashes. Their young brood had left them for a while, and were feeding in the apple-trees.

Here, then, were these two, perched side by side, wearing an expression of perfect content. It seemed to me that they were reviewing together the hopes and struggles of the spring just vanished. Did they talk of the storms which the nest had weathered and the hawks that had sought in vain? Were they swelling with pride over the family which they had reared, and especially in such cold, wet weather?

I do know, though I cannot read their thoughts, that before their family joined them again the male bird raised his bill to his mate's, caressing her with all the affection of sincere and simple courtship.

As we passed a stack-yard the house-martins were almost as busy as ever. I thought I heard the voices of young birds proceeding from a nest. If, however, a cold snap suddenly descends, the nest will be a tomb and not a cradle.

In the valley the starlings were massing. The hundreds that I saw will soon be thousands. They will flash in the evening sun and chatter bewilderingly. Then comes the sudden hush that tells of purple heads being thrust into pillows of sable feathers.

Along one of the lanes we came across Jerry. He was carrying a dead rabbit, and, after the usual greetings, I lifted the animal to see whether a tell-tale line around the neck indicated the work of a wire snare.

Jerry smiled and shook his head. "Not this time," he said, pointing to a small puncture which showed itself at the base of the ears.

213

"Stoat," he said, laconically.

"How do you know it wasn't a weasel's work?" I asked.

"Saw it," he answered, just as curtly. "As a matter of fact," he continued, "weasels are not very often seen. At least, they do not show themselves as much as stoats. They are underground animals. They love to travel through the burrows of mice and moles, and you generally see 'em as they dart across the lane. It's a young rabbit, though full grown."

I took hold of bunny again to see whether I could have told its age, but, finding no certain signs of youth save for the light fawn colour behind his ears, I said:

"Are you certain it's a young one?"

For answer the old poacher took one of the ears between his thumb and finger, and, pulling a little, I saw the skin tear easily.

"If ye want to know whether a rabbit is a young 'un or not, test it like that," he said. "If it's an old 'un or a tough old buck, ye'll not find the ear will tear as easily as this one's did.'

As we walked along I noticed that Raq was not sampling the hedges and bushes as he usually did, but kept walking behind my companion. He kept moving his head from side to side, and every now and then he raised his nose in the air. It was not the dangling rabbit that he was following. Just as I was on the point of mentioning his behaviour to my companion, Jerry laughed and touched his inside pocket.

He unbuttoned his coat, and in its depths I at once saw the gleam of bronze and gold.

"That dog o' your'n is enough to give any one away to a sharp-eyed keeper," he said. "He's bin gettin' the whiff o' this bird fer some time, though he's bin a bit puzzled as to where it is."

"And how did you come by it?" I asked, as sternly as befitted my station. "Did a stoat nip that in the neck too?"

Jerry did not answer for a moment or two, and then he said:

"As a matter o' fact, I've got a merciful streak in my natur'. There was a shoot here yesterday, and that allus means that there are wounded birds left aboot that seek oot quiet places to die in. Some of 'em hang out alive for a day or two, but the end is allus pretty certain — a prowlin' fox, a wanderin' stoat, or the sure rat."

He looked at me, and, seeing the look of disapproval fading from my face, he continued:

"I allus make it a point to wander over the fields when the pheasant drive is finished. I don't like to think o' wounded birds waitin' for slow death to ovvertak' 'em. This is one on 'em," he said, tapping his inside pocket. "I rather think he was a rocketer."

"A what?" I queried.

"A rocketer. Never heerd on't?" he asked.

I shook my head, and, turning in towards a gate, Jerry indicated where he had found the dead bird. "A long way from where any o' the guns were posted," he added.

I forbore to question, as I saw he was going to piece together the story of the bird's death.

"The birds would be comin' ovver," he said, "and the guns would be poppin' off on all sides. Most o' the birds would be flyin' just ovver the tops o' the trees, makin' good shootin'."

I nodded appreciatively. In my mind's eye I could see them streaming from their cover, full of life, beauty, energy, only to be met by a blast of leaden hail — then to crumple up and thud to the ground.

"But this one, I fancy," continued my companion, "must a bin a more difficult shot. It must a bin high up, and the sportsman took aim and pulled trigger on the off-chance of a bullet findin' its billet."

Here he pulled the dead bird from its hiding place and gave it to me to examine.

"Not a shot mark aboot it," he remarked. "Might be unharmed."

"It has a broken wing," I said.

"I'm comin' to that," said Jerry curtly.

"Well," continued my companion, "o' the scores o' shot that rattled around it, one did its work. Found a vital spot, but not enough to bring it to the ground immediately.

"The bird felt the shock, but struggled gamely on, its one thought to make for yon spinney that ye see there behind the stubble-field. But suddenly it lost all sense o' direction. The landscape faded from its view, and, like the last flare-up of a flickerin' wick, there came one last spurt o' furious life, and, knowin' not what it was doin' or where it was goin', only knowin' that it must keep its wings movin', it started to tower."

216

I looked at Jerry to interpret, and, after moving his hand horizontally (and as he did so I saw he was imitating the bird's flight), his hand, with its first finger raised, began to travel upwards as straight as a rocket towards the sky.

"Up and up went the bird, with life fast ebbin' away."

"How high?" I asked breathlessly.

"Perhaps a couple o' hundred yards or more," Jerry answered, "until he had no strength to travel any higher — just strength enough to spread oot his bonny wings like a parachute. For a second or two he managed to keep 'em oppen, then he came down like this" — and Jerry raised his hand, and, as it spiralled downwards, I could see the gallant bird with outstretched wings descending in circles of increasing speed.

"When he was fifty yards from t' ground the bullet finished its work. His splendid head drooped forrards, the wings collapsed, and like a stone he fell dead where I found 'im. That's 'ow his wing came to be broke."

We were silent for a moment or two. Over the stubble-field a lark rose, and sprayed the pleasant land with a few drops of song.

"And if ye'd like to tak' 'im with ye," said Jerry, handing me the bird, "ye'll find one bullet embedded in 'is little brain — only one, but it was one too many."

"And no bird ever had finer obituary," I said, squeezing his arm affectionately, and, though my companion made no comment, yet I knew he liked his descriptions to be appreciated. Who does not?

"By the way," I said, just before we parted. "Why didn't you carry your pheasant alongside of your rabbit? Why did you stow one away in your pocket and dangle the other for all to see?"

He did not answer at once: then his face wreathed into a smile.

"Once upon a time," said he, "there were two on us shootin' rabbits with the help o' ferrets. I had a gun licence — my companion hadn't. It were the only one I ever 'ad, and I must a got it when I weren't thinking. Suddenly up looms a policeman and comes ovver to us."

"Rather awkward," I said.

"I had just time, before I bolted, to tell my pal to stand still, and the bobby started to come after me," Jerry continued.

"But —" I commenced. Jerry silenced me with a wave of his hand and went on:

"After being chased fer a couple o' fields, I slowed down, and the bobby came up and asked me fer my licence. So I showed it to him, and when he had seen that it was genuine he said angrily, 'But what did yer run away fer?' So I told him that I always took a bit o' exercise when ferretin', as it was cold work standin' aboot."

"Meanwhile," I said, finishing the yarn for him, "the other fellow, who hadn't a licence, got away."

"That's aboot it," Jerry said, with a broad grin. "And if I walk with a rabbit openly and meet t' keeper, he's so busy askin' about t' rabbit which he can see, and knows I've found quite genuine-like, that t'other feller in t' pocket gets away scot-free."

We parted then, and as I left him he called out, "So ye'll no take the bird wi' ye?"

I shook my head. "No, thanks," I called back, "it would need too much explaining. Besides, I have no rabbit to dangle." And with that Raq and I turned homewards.

The lanes were being carpeted with golden leaves. The hedges flashed with gold, purple, crimson. As I looked at them Jerry's description of the final effort of the towering bird came to my mind — " A last spurt o' furious life." Yes! that is what seemed to be happening round about me. Nature was rocketing to its apex of gorgeous colour — then sleep.

Also available in ISIS Large Print:

Walking In My Sleep

Jane Chichester

Untroubled by any formal education or adult supervision, Jane fills her days with her animals, imaginary companions and the eccentric people who live or work on the farm. She observes her glamorous parents's parties with a critical eye, but they are not part of her life.

When war breaks out, this peaceful existence is shattered by the arrival of a family of female cousins who move in for the duration. They bring with them a governess and, therefore, discipline, timetables and regular meals. This enchanting book, sometimes sad and sometimes hilarious, tells how she comes to terms with an invasion which she sees as bad as any going on across the Channel.

ISBN 0-7531-9322-1 (hb)
ISBN 0-7531-9323-X (pb)

A Romany on the Trail

G. Bramwell Evens

Romany is back on the trail in another collection of tales from the countryside. He draws us into fellowship with the fur and feather folk of hedgerow and heath, field and river-bank, wood and moor, and he shows us hidden wonder and hidden meaning.

From glorious pine forests with carpets of needles, to early lambs and night fishing, we share all of Romany and Raq's experiences. We also meet their friends, Jerry the Poacher, Sally Stordy, Ned the village postman and many others.

ISBN 0-7531-9314-0 (hb)
ISBN 0-7531-9315-9 (pb)